ENDO1

Leon Johnson has written his personal story, a self-assessment, and a testimony of the power of God's Word to transform his life in his book, Your Rescued Life: Ten Keys to Transformational Peace. Over and over again, he demonstrates that "right thinking" based on the power of the Word, can transform a life. He is a disciple who makes disciples. His aim is that every aspect of how one lives is shaped by how one believes. He gives tried and true examples from his own life, and from the testimony of others of the transforming power of the Word. I would recommend this book to those who would long to learn how to apply the Word of God to their deepest thinking. Rev. Dr. David Chotka, Chair, Alliance Pray Team (C&MA Canada), Author and Conference Speaker

Leon Johnson has given us a great gift in writing, Your Rescued Life: Ten Keys to Transformational Peace. Counselors tell us being honest with deep hurts from childhood is one of the toughest things with which people have to deal. And, the same counselors tell us that what we keep hidden is what keeps us ill. Leon is to be commended for his honesty about his own life. He is to be commended for his gentle, understanding and compassionate treatment of others who have suffered similar pain. The Biblical and clear path of direction he spells out will help others suffering with these self-identity issues. —Rev. Dr. John Vawter, Past President, Phoenix Seminary and Western Seminary

In Your Rescued Life: Ten Keys to Transformational Peace, Leon Johnson offers an intensely personal memoir of learning to confront false and harmful thoughts with the truth of God's Word and the voice of the Holy Spirit. If you have struggled to find self-worth, a positive outlook, and a healthy inner life, let this veteran teacher show you what he has learned. —Joseph Castleberry, Pd.D., President of Northwest University and author of Your Deepest Dream: Discovering God's True Vision for Your Life

When Leon Johnson was growing up, he discovered it was hard to make friends with his peers. Sometimes, he was bullied and called names. Many can relate to these experiences. His inner voice told him he did not measure up, causing deep insecurity. Your Rescued Life: Ten Keys to Transformational Peace describes the inspiring journey of how Leon overcame the damaging effect of his negative inner voice. Now he sees his true value. His story and the ten keys he provides will make a difference in your life. — Elliott Katz, author of Being the Strong Man A Woman Wants: Timeless Wisdom on Being a Man

Leon Johnson gives the reader key principles to live by in order to eliminate negative thinking and pessimistic words about ourselves in his book, Your Rescued Life: Ten Keys to Transformational Peace. These truths will change your life when you realize who you are in Christ and constantly remind yourself how God views you. The enemy of our souls relentlessly accuses us, tells us lies, and endeavors to discourage us. Jesus Christ is just the opposite as he encourages us, forgives us, and tells us the truth. As you read this book, follow Leon's principles, and you will never be the same. —Dr. Wayde Goodall Vice President, Hope Education Network Convoy of Hope Strategic Pastoral Advisor Focus on the Family

YOUR RESCUED LIFE

TEN KEYS TO

TRANSFORMATIONAL PEACE

BY LEON JOHNSON

ISBN 978-1-7363633-0-0

Endurance Publishing Company

Puyallup, WA

OTHER AVAILABLE PRODUCTS & SERVICES

Discussion Guide

ISBN: 978-1-7363633-1-7

Audiobook

ISBN: 978-1-7363633-2-4

eBook

ISBN: 978-1-7363633-3-1

4-Compact Disks Set

ISBN: 978-1-7363633-4-8

Seminar speaker and teacher available upon request

Leon@YourRescuedLife.com

DEDICATION

For my dear wife, for her love, dedication and patience

For our wonderful family

TABLE OF CONTENTS

PREFACE

You may have heard it said that hindsight is 20/20. That's certainly how it's been for me. The longer we continue to live, the more acute our understanding of how and why our life has unfolded as it has. One would think that as life evolves, we would get better and better at living life. That isn't necessarily so. And that's the reason I finally gave in to the Holy Spirit to write after a year of refusing. This is my story of spiritual transformation made possible by the power of the Scriptures and the ministry of the Holy Spirit. My goal is to help the reader discover how to live in the freedom God intended for us as a disciple of our Lord Jesus.

INTRODUCTION

My mission is to help people aged thirteen through adulthood, to discover how to live in the freedom of really knowing and loving themselves, to develop a healthy inner language and to live boldly knowing they are enough.

Stop and think about your own inner voice. What common thread in your inner language have you used over time that has shaped the person you've become? Does your inner voice speak truth or lies? Have you spent so much time listening to your inner voice that you believe these thoughts whether true or not?

This book is the link connector between children's self-identity and the developed language they adopt as their own. Through the lens of the Scriptures, readers will learn a new positive way to think about who they are, how to identify and value their personal gifts and talents and how to use their newfound boldness to connect and serve others.

The topics covered offer an in-depth understanding of what transpires when words, environment and personality collide in unhealthy ways. Then I offer positive, practical ways of viewing oneself differently—literally by transforming the way we think. It's an immutable (unchangeable) principle I adopted that led me to a place of peace for my inner man.

Your Rescued Life will teach readers:

- how to have a positive attitude about yourself.
- how the inner words spoken in childhood can dramatically affect daily life.
- how to forgive those who have perhaps hurt them.
- how to see themselves as God sees them as described in the Scriptures.
- how to forgive yourself and gain transformational peace

At the end of each chapter, watch for the immutable (unchangeable) principle that author, Leon Johnson adopted that led him to a place of peace for his inner man.

To get us started, I invite you to go for a walk with me. Not just any walk, but to a place where we see an eight-year-old blond, freckled boy standing in a mostly straight line with other boys and girls on the newly mown baseball field behind Denmark School*, an old brick building with a pitched roof and bold brick columns capped with concrete squares at its entrance.

Do you see him? As lunch recess unfolds on a warm spring day, imagine the baseball teams being formed one by one. He's still just standing there waiting—waiting to be selected for a team. His body stiffens as he nervously pushes his hands deeper into his pockets. And finally, it happens. The lone boy is finally chosen by default. Do you see the downcast look on his face? See the disappointment in his eyes as he meanders toward his new team without much enthusiasm? He doesn't realize he's reinforcing how his classmates perceive him. Can you imagine the words he's repeating in his mind? "Pick me! I want a chance!" This isn't his first baseball game either. And each game increases his negative self-talk. He wonders what's wrong with him. His inner voice is growing louder and louder each time it speaks.

The next day, rather than play baseball, the boy decides to choose the tall, old-fashioned swings hanging from long metal chains with a wide leather strap for a seat. This choice causes virtually no anxiety. "No one has to choose me here. I can swing as high and fast as I want," he thinks to himself. Unknowingly, that decision further separates him from his peers.

CHAPTER 1

CONFLICT WITHIN
Laying the Groundwork

An exuberant, almost rowdy bunch of five- and six-year-old boys and girls returned to their first-grade classroom after the lunch recess bell ended their play. The after-lunch rest requirement had automatically begun as students filtered back into the classroom after stopping at the drinking fountain in the main hall leading to the playground.

To that end, each student picked up a colorful inch-thick quilted mat from the neatly stacked pile of perhaps thirty mats. No one thought about whether those mats were dirty or not. Day after day, they were thrown on the floor with everyone else's recess dirt still on them. No one ever chose the same mat twice.

Mrs. Nieves, a soft-spoken, older, blonde-haired woman must have been grateful for a quiet time to calm us down so we'd be ready to learn again. Sometimes a student would go to sleep, and she would just let him sleep. Mrs. Nieves told my mom at a parent/teacher conference that sometimes students weren't getting enough sleep at home, which was why it was so vital that we rested for at least fifteen minutes on the gritty, hardwood floor.

Like everyone else, I was always on the hunt for empty floor space to lay my mat, aiming for a space next to the cutest first-grade girl. Day after day I tried to place my mat next to hers, but, unfortunately, others had gotten there first. Girls jockeyed for places near other girls, and most boys found space nearer to boys than to girls. I didn't learn until much later that girls think boys are yucky at that age. My dad and mom were friends with that cute girl's parents, and I loved going to their house for short visits.

Mrs. Nieves was a really nice lady. She was probably a good teacher too, but as an immature first-grade boy, I couldn't really know. But day after day she taught me to write and do math problems. I don't recall having any problems adapting to school. Nor do I remember thinking I was different from any other student. I wouldn't discover that until the third grade. What's that saying? "What you don't know can't hurt you." But that's not necessarily true. At the end of the year, I was promoted to second grade.

When I think back to those early school years, I was simply unaware of many things—perhaps not yet ready to learn as the youngest student in my class. Kindergartens didn't exist back then, so I was only five when I entered first grade. My late October birthday didn't prevent my parents from enrolling me, because that's how it was done back then. I didn't know until later that only one other student was my age. The rest of the class was at least six, and some were an entire year older than I. In hindsight, I think it would have been wise for this little boy to have waited until the following year to begin school.

We lived on a farm in a weathered, old, white two-story farmhouse a country block from Denmark School. Only a lush, green

 pasture separated our farm from the school where all four of the Johnson kids went to primary school. When my parents had two children, they believed their family was complete. Then, due to poor family planning or God's providence, I was born eight years after my oldest brother and five years after my only sister. Dad told me decades later that my birth was a surprise, as was that of my brother who was three years younger than I. I have tried to imagine how my mother felt when she realized she was pregnant again after my sister was born. Did she accept the pregnancy or was she discouraged at the thought of bringing

another baby into the family? When I was eleven, my older brother got married, and three years after that, my sister went off to college in Seattle. That left only my brother and me at home with our parents. It's hard to even remember much more than the six of us sitting around the dinner table. Back then Dad worked ten- to sixteen-hour days managing both our dairy and farming 160 acres, so during those early years, Dad left most of the child rearing to mom.

As a child, most of the time I spent with my dad was on Sunday mornings. Like clockwork, everyone would dress in their Sunday best to go to church. Dad's assignment was to call me into  the bathroom, pick up the tapered black barber's comb, and comb my hair. He'd firmly hold my chin with his left hand and use his right to comb it. It was something I looked forward to each week—my one point of personal contact with him during those early years. As my younger brother and I grew older, we spent much more time with our dad. He taught us how to milk cows in the dairy barn and run farm equipment in our fields. There were always about twenty-five to thirty Holsteins as well as an occasional Guernsey or Ayrshire in the herd that needed to be milked morning and evening. The work was never done. I'm grateful that Dad modeled a good work ethic, which has since served me well.

We lived ten miles from town, so Sunday after church was one of the few times we had a chance to interact with other children. Of course, not much play was permitted there, but sometimes we'd go to someone's house in town after the evening church service where we always had a great time playing tag or hide-and-seek. With so little in the way of socialization, it's no wonder I was inexperienced when I finally went to school.

Thinking back, I realize now that, beginning in second grade, certain student groups were already forming based on personality, power, popularity, athletic ability and even socioeconomic status. Research and experience indicate that no matter the age, social setting and/or work environment, natural leaders emerge and let the rest of us know who is in control. And though I didn't understand what was happening at the time, life was already teaching me about social structures.

In second grade, I was still the youngest student at six, while most everyone else had already turned seven. It would always be like that for me. All the Johnson kids had fall birthdays and graduated from high school when we were just seventeen. It makes you wonder what farmers do in the dead of winter!

That year was memorable for learning subtraction facts and playing rhythm sticks in sync with the piano played by my classroom teacher, Mrs. Hawks. She was a warm, wonderful, slightly-built woman who played like no one I'd ever heard before. It was absolutely great to play rhythm sticks with my class to happy, syncopated songs. She would break the song every eight measures while the rhythm sticks maintained the beat and tempo. Part of the fun included performing at Denmark School's festive Christmas concerts. I'll never forget the red velvet stage curtain opening to reveal my second-grade class ready to perform. I'll always fondly remember looking over the edge of the stage to see and hear Mrs. Hawks accompany her enthusiastic little performers. Second grade brought greater clarity regarding social structures, but for some reason, I never quite fit into a circle of friends. I was promoted to third grade with no understanding of what was yet to come.

I began taking piano lessons from Mrs. Hawks that year. I had already developed a love for music, perhaps from hearing her play. She had an ebony upright Steinway piano in her home that was like driving a car with a V-8 engine. Even as an eight-year-old, I loved improvising as we played simple duets together. My parents, I'm grateful to say, literally sacrificed for my sister and me to have half-hour lessons for $2 each back in the fifties and sixties. I continued to visit and play for Mrs. Hawks in her home well into adulthood. Because she gave me the gift of music, it was a sad day for me when she passed away.

In third grade, I learned cursive writing and multiplication facts, got the mumps and discovered more about comparing myself to others. My teacher was Mrs. Gibb, a kind, middle-aged farmer's wife. I also learned some hard lessons about how tough it is for some of us to make friends. For some, making friends seemed effortless, depending on their popularity and athletic abilities or other interests. But I was into music and had little interest in sports. I did enjoy baseball, but as I mentioned earlier, my enthusiasm was dashed when I was constantly chosen last. Did you ever have the sense that something was wrong, but you just couldn't put your finger on it? At that point, there was definitely something going on that I could not yet see or hear. Everything seemed to be going well until, suddenly, it wasn't. I realized more and more that I wasn't the popular, well-rounded boy I hoped for—not in sports, not in making friends, not in having good looks and certainly not being at the top of my class. At least that's how it seemed.

My bus ride to school was a forty-five-minute route to neighboring farms to pick up other students, even though the school was just across the pasture from my house. The Kittitas Valley has always been a beautiful place. The flourishing farms there grew different crops—mostly wheat, oats, Timothy hay, potatoes and corn. Several farms also included a dairy farm like ours. Farm kids tend to learn early about a work ethic. It was my dad's work ethic that motivated me to finish college, so let me encourage you—never give up.

One day, a popular boy in my class got on the bus at his regular stop. He headed straight back to sit with me, holding his baseball glove in his hand. I was glad he chose my seat. I don't remember what we talked about, though it seemed normal enough. But at the next stop, another student got on the bus, and my seatmate moved to sit with him.

I felt that I must be inadequate compared to the other student if he preferred his company to mine. I know he had no intention of making me feel unworthy. Who thinks like that at eight years of age? The truth is that my own inner voice jumped to conclusions based on what I felt. Unfortunately, perceptions can sometimes lie.

I was often the last student chosen for organized play, and each time, I'd review in my mind the negative inner self-talk that led me even further away from believing I had value. "You're not like other kids. You can't do things as well as other kids. You're not as smart as other kids. You're not very good looking." Experiences like that will touch our emotions and never be forgotten.

A teacher actually told my mom that I was a boy whose lights were on, but there was nobody home—a reference to my intelligence and attention span. I was heartbroken as I listened to my mom repeat that story to her friends, further driving my negative inner language into overdrive. Why would she do that? I found myself replaying these things over and over in my head until I believed the lies that I was deficient—worthless.

That year my mom went to a Valentine's Day planning meeting with two or three other room mothers. Mom was so humiliated by one very stylish and somewhat beautiful mother who asked, "What are we going to do with you—stand you in a corner?" Mom came home and repeated the story, obviously badly hurt. I felt her pain as if it had been passed on to me—that I'd been inextricably linked to my mother—and later in life, that my mother's obesity was now my obesity. I wondered if there was something wrong with our family. My inner negative language was increasing exponentially.

I was promoted to fourth grade, the last grade offered at Denmark School. Mrs. McQueen played the double role of teacher and principal. That meant she was in and out of the classroom sometimes for principal duties. A student room monitor was assigned to write on the blackboard the names of those who were misbehaving while she was gone. Mrs. McQueen was a stern woman, probably in her fifties, who walked briskly in her business attire as if to announce she was in charge. We were introduced to geography and social studies, long division and report writing. It's not surprising that I was still haunted by always being chosen last for playground games.

One day, Mrs. McQueen ordered all twelve or thirteen fourth grade boys into the boys' bathroom and stood squarely in front of the urinals. Wow—a woman in the boys' bathroom! I was terribly embarrassed to be in the bathroom with a woman, especially this one—the principal. We gathered into a tight group, standing at attention as we listened to Mrs. McQueen's foreboding voice. She moved to a urinal to demonstrate what it should look like when boys go to the bathroom. "Someone is urinating on the walls, and it's got to stop," she warned. "Now let me show you how you're supposed to use these urinals. You stand squarely in front of them like this, and go directly into the urinal—no spraying around on the walls," she ordered, as she placed both of her hands on either side of the front of her skirt, letting us know boys were different from girls. I thought to myself, guys pee on walls sometimes. I must have been pretty naive. It never occurred to me that it was possible or even reasonable to do so.

I was promoted to fifth grade and then on to middle school in Kittitas the following year. Suffice it to say not much changed about how I felt about myself. Name-calling was sometimes bothersome, but I usually deflected it using my extroverted personality and sense of humor. One day during summer break, I was walking back to the house after finishing my chores, past our dilapidated green doghouse. I was both humiliated and hurt when I saw that someone had sneaked into our yard and spray-painted the word Tanker on the side— comparing my weight to a Sherman tank. I was even more upset to know I would never forget it.

During those middle school years, I told myself mental lies that hindered me from attempting to make friends with other kids. I was confused, realizing that with my outgoing personality and humor, I should've easily been able to make friends. But it didn't happen. Looking back, it's clear that no one had ever equipped me with encouraging words that would inspire me to leave behind the negative input of the past. Perhaps it would've been different had I been taught a few strategies that could help me fit in. I suppose I could have asked for help, but it never occurred to me. For example, I might have used affirmations to help me see and believe how God sees and loves me. Still, I have some positive memories of eighth grade, graduating from middle school, and moving on to high school.

I have some really good memories of high school—where I succeeded in some classes and struggled in others. I was enrolled in choral music all four years and took piano lessons from Mrs. Hawks on Saturdays. I had good friends, though most were girls because the emphasis for the guys in our high school was on sports, especially basketball. Since I was into music, wasn't particularly athletically gifted and was somewhat overweight, I struggled to find anything in common with the other guys. I often overheard them discussing their weekend conquests, alcohol consumption and smoking, all of which were taboo in our family. My family's faith also prohibited going to theaters and dances.

While I was in high school, one of the more popular guys invited me to see The Sound of Music at the theater. What? A musical? What a thought! But, of course, when I asked, my mom refused to let me go. It was a huge disappointment. This boy was always friendly toward me and would have made a good friend, but our friendship never developed because I couldn't go to the movie. My dad had gone to the theater on John Deere Day to see a film about John Deere manufacturing and equipment, so I couldn't understand the reason why I couldn't go see the movie. I could see nothing evil in The Sound of Music.

When the school yearbook was released at the end of my junior year, I was surprised to see I had been voted as Best All Around. That felt great until I heard that it meant round as in obese. At the time, I was nearly six feet tall and weighed 192 pounds, so I didn't think of myself as a really heavy person, but kids can be cruel. It's possible I really had been voted best all around. Many students and teachers liked me and seemed to enjoy my sense of humor.

One day, after the bell rang in junior English, one of the guys in my class, a somewhat cocky guy with a personality to match, followed me to my locker. He abruptly spun me around, grabbed me by the front of my shirt and slammed me up against my locker, causing a loud crash that drew a crowd of other students who began to yell, "Fight, fight!" He swore at me and accused me of something, but I couldn't understand what he said in the heat of the moment. I should have punched him, but I was taught not to fight or I would risk consequences at home. All I had left was my inner voice that trapped me and left me feeling both helpless and hopeless. From this vantage point, I wonder what motivated him to single me out. Perception is truth to the person perceiving it. I wish I had known how to explore and claim the real truth when I was younger.

Those memories have replayed in my head many times, but there were many good times too, like when I used my sense of humor to make people laugh with corny jokes and plays on words. As an adult, I've often wondered if I used humor as a coping mechanism. Some girls and a few guys both at school and at church became my good friends, but we didn't hang around together because our farm was three miles from school and ten miles from church.

Early on, my siblings and I knew better than to ask our mom certain things. We heard no a lot when we asked to do things. Later in life, I wondered if there was more to it than just her negative, protective nature—money was scarce in those days. Still, there were a lot of rules, and experience taught us it was better not to break them.

I'd like to share another story to help you better understand the emotions behind a lack of self-acceptance. This is the story of a friend of mine, a middle-aged woman I'll call June:

"I was called the freckle-faced little girl...the ugly, little, redheaded girl with whom no one wanted to be friends. That voice stayed with me well into my teenage years where I had to learn to paint my face, wear high-heeled shoes, wear revealing clothing and fix my hair really big. I did it to get the attention of others. Then and only then did I feel like I could fit in with my peers. But my inner voice was always telling me how ugly, skinny, and unattractive I was—and such a failure. These same thoughts and voices followed me into adulthood. I had multiple marriages and resorted to alcoholism. I repeatedly tried to find happiness, dull the pain and silence the voices. It was not until I found Jesus that the healing began. Though I'm still a work in progress, I began to love myself. I can still hear those negative voices occasionally. It is still my mom's positive affirmations I choose to hold onto rather than my negative inner voice. I was delivered from those negative voices. I'm now learning how to hear God's voice better each day. Now that is cool!"

Thanks for sharing your personal story, June.

Though I received countless affirmations for all I'd accomplished as an adult, I couldn't receive the affirmations as truth, because I didn't believe they applied to me. I failed to understand and accept the person God created me to be. From whom was I trying to gain approval? How many accomplishments would it take to be enough?

It's taken practically a lifetime to unravel who I really am. My life, career and family played out very successfully, though I never took the time to unpack the inner emotional pain I carried. I just never dealt with it. I never really examined why I felt like I didn't fit in. The pain was deeply buried, so I never understood the underlying messages that were still impacting me.

Finally, I faced a significant spiritual battle as well as a deep emotional healing. During a three-week period, the Holy Spirit brought powerful, life-changing Scripture to my memory each day, accompanied by the theological lyrics of a hymn that seemed to match the lesson of the Scripture for that day. It was as if God was dismantling my religion and rebuilding my faith. Even so, I still failed to take care of the underlying causes of my emotional pain.

As an adult, I often asked my parents what it was like to grow up in the 1920s and 1930s. Dad was quiet and very introverted, and Mom was outgoing and shared her opinion freely, even if you didn't want to hear it. However, neither would talk about their childhood. I hoped to compare their childhood experiences to my own to see if there was some kind of traumatic connection that had somehow been passed on to me through epigenetics.

Epigenetics is the study of gene expression when a person experiences trauma as a result of something that happened in a previous generation; e.g., psychological, sexual, financial, accident, death, to name a few. It's not that our genes change. When trauma is experienced, the gene expressed from that trauma has potential to pass on that same trauma to the next generation. In his book, *It Didn't Start With You,* author Mark Wolynn, Director of The Family Constellation Institute in San Francisco, explained how he scientifically proved there is an epigenetic link that helps to shape who we are when gene expression is altered by trauma. In several cases, his epigenetic research conclusively showed the link to inherited trauma. He demonstrated how this trauma can be passed down through multiple generations that may result in a variety of psychological problems. It's a startling study coinciding with Numbers 14:18. (Other passages cited include Exodus 20:5 and Exodus 34:6-7.) "The Lord is slow to anger and filled with unfailing love, forgiving every kind of sin and rebellion. But he does not excuse the guilty. He lays the sins of the parents upon their children; the entire family is affected—even children in the third and fourth generations."

I remember three different significant events clearly involving my dad, after my wife and I had been married for several years. He told me in the driveway at the farm that I was just different from my two brothers. Another negative hit. What did he mean by that? Had I disappointed him? He had a difficult time relating to me, perhaps because of our completely opposite personalities and interests. My older and younger brothers were both very athletic. My younger brother had set local, regional and state records in basketball. Interestingly enough, Dad wasn't athletic, but appreciated sports and admired my brothers' accomplishments. My siblings and I believe Dad felt sad because he hadn't finished school beyond eighth grade. In his defense, life was just different in the 1920s and 1930s in the Midwest where he lived before moving to Washington at seventeen. Their lives were agriculturally based, which meant children sometimes quit school and went to work on the farm because they had to. Neither my dad or mom's life growing up could have been easy since they both implied they were from poor families and had very little in the way of relationships with their own parents. Mom's dad passed away when she was just sixteen years old.

The second truly significant thing was the day dad told me he was proud of all that I had accomplished in my career. I launched a successful home-based audio/video productions business, becoming Technology Director and Special Programs Administrator at my school district, and learned a great deal about computing, video production and other technologies. It was truly a red-letter day for me when Dad said that. As you can imagine, my inner self-talk began to morph toward the positive as a result.

Lastly, after my dad retired from the farm and moved to western Washington, he told me he loved me. Then he awkwardly hugged me. Poor, quiet Dad nearly choked as he spoke words that didn't come easily for him, but hugs became more frequent whenever we visited after that happened.

My siblings and I knew our parents loved us; there was no question about that. We were an intact, fairly functional family. But verbal expression of that love was quite another thing. Again, it's very likely that my parents rarely heard affirmations or received physical affection. And if that's the case, they would have struggled to pass those on to their own children. It simply wasn't natural or comfortable for them to do that. For me, this resulted in a negative self-perception. In fact, I believe many people are struggling with self-image because they were never affirmed or nurtured as children.

Author Ted Dekker[1] sets the record straight in his book, The Forgotten Way:

"The lie that you cannot measure up will create a terrible anxiety gap deep in your heart. This subconscious, insidious fear creates the feeling of vast separation between you and your Heavenly Father. God is staggering in His precision and completion. Nothing about you remotely resembles a mistake. If you were the only human alive, He would be flowing with rivers of love and pride in you and for you."

Have you ever thought about how you're able to remember some things but not others? I've come to this conclusion—what we remember best are the words and events that have touched our emotions. I find it interesting that my wife and I remember different things about the same event. Sometimes neither of us remembers much at all about an event. I tend to mentally record memories of those events that are relatable. Most of the rest are forgotten.

We all have memories that are both great and terrible, and a few mediocre memories can even pop up now and then. But most of the rest of life's memories are forgotten because those events rang no emotional bell inside us. This makes me want to truly grasp the difference between knowing God and really experiencing God. I've had many uplifting experiences in the presence of the Holy Spirit throughout my adult life. I've often felt deeply moved to be teaching at church, directing choirs and playing the piano to glorify the Father who is in Heaven. We should never minimize such positive experiences. In fact, Scripture says it's good to remember and count the blessings of God in our lives, because they build and strengthen our faith.

But those things are no longer enough. Since that time, I've discovered another level of relationship entirely, a relationship where we can be in much deeper communion with Him, sharing our hearts with Him in the secret place. It's getting to know Jesus, practicing what the Scriptures teach and recognizing the impressions or gentle whisper of the Holy Spirit and obeying what He says. I'm in no way saying I've arrived. I'm simply a lifelong learner, eager to know Jesus on a deeper level and to understand His heart. During this learning process, I discovered the vast difference between doing and being. God loves us regardless.

When God reaches us, we remember—His grace and forgiveness, His love and presence with us each day and His ability to change us into His likeness. It's a slow process, or at least it has been for me. But the process has been a beautiful thing. When we experience God, He touches our emotions, and that helps us remember who we are—we are His beloved children. We remember, and we forget. My hope is for more remembering and less forgetting. Jesus has the solution written in John 14:26-27: "But when the Father sends the Advocate as my representative—that is, the Holy Spirit—he will teach you everything and will remind you of everything I have told you. I am leaving you with a gift—peace of mind and heart. And the peace I give is a gift the world cannot give. So, don't be troubled or afraid."

Let's distinguish between what I believe to be the difference between the Holy Spirit reaching our emotions and/or becoming emotional. They're really two different things. Remember what I shared previously regarding our event memories? It's that moment the light bulb goes on in our heads. The Scriptures speak relevance to our lives, offering us an aha moment for the very first time. The truth is that I've read certain portions of the Bible many times, yet, the very next time, I could suddenly see something for the very first time.

I'll share a great example from Ephesians 3:20. "Now all glory to God, who is able, through his mighty power at work within us, to accomplish infinitely more than we might ask or think." All of a sudden, as I read, the phrase "through his mighty power at work within us" leapt off the page. I couldn't get away from it. It connected to my understanding and expanded my thinking in a new way. I'd been reading over the top of that phrase for years, but had I been asked to quote it from memory, I would have left out one of the most important parts of the verse.

It's also possible to become emotional during those moments. It happened to Paul, the Apostle, in Ephesians 3. He had just explained in verses 1-13 the incredible power of Jesus to forgive us of our sins—the plan of salvation—God's grace applied to our souls. As he reflected on how Jesus had transformed him, Paul became overwhelmed by the thought as explained in verses 14 through 19: "When I think of all this, I fall to my knees and pray to the Father, the Creator of everything in heaven and on earth. I pray that from his glorious, unlimited resources he will empower you with inner strength through his Spirit. Then Christ will make his home in your hearts as you trust in him. Your roots will grow down into God's love and keep you strong. And may you have the power to understand, as all God's people should, how wide, how long, how high, and how deep his love is. May you experience the love of Christ, though it is too great to understand fully. Then you will be made complete with all the fullness of life and power that comes from God."

IMMUTABLE PRINCIPLE #1: I will learn to love and accept myself as I am. We must confront old lies with the truth of who God created us to be—not the things we chose to believe while we were young. I will start with acknowledging and grieving the past for what it was and then leave it behind. Scripture says that I am already enough.

In Matthew 22:37-40, "Jesus replied, 'You must love the Lord your God with all your heart, all your soul, and all your mind. This is the first and greatest commandment. A second is equally important:

Love your neighbor as yourself.' The entire law and all the demands of the prophets are based on these two commandments."

IMMUTABLE PRINCIPLE #2: I am determined that I will thoughtfully review even the most familiar Scriptures cited in this book.

Colossians 3:16 tells us, "Let the word of Christ dwell (reside) in you richly, teaching and admonishing one another in all wisdom, singing psalms and hymns and spiritual songs, with thankfulness in your hearts to God."

PRAYER: Father, I pray in Jesus' holy name that You will search my heart and expose the reasons that I feel I'm not good enough. I ask You to show me what I need to grieve, then heal my emotions and set me on the path of life You have planned for me. Help me to value the power of Your Word and Holy Spirit in my life. Amen.

The truth of who we are is in knowing and understanding how God sees us. In the following chapters, we will explore the Scriptures that identify who we really are. Hint: We are God's masterpiece.

There is hope ahead.

CHAPTER 2

BUCKETS OF WORDS

Old Language – Sticks and Stones

Just last week, my wife and I received a text from our daughter in another state. Not much gets by our very verbal eight-year-old grandson. Our daughter had simply used the words *"quite a few"* in a couple of short sentences. Sounds innocent enough, doesn't it? It's not an uncommon phrase, but what followed next caused us to laugh. Our grandson exclaimed, *"You sound just like Grandma."* And he didn't just say it once; he said it every time she said *"quite a few"*. In order to memorialize that moment for all time, our four-year-old granddaughter wanted to make a video to send to her grandma. *"This is how Grandma talks,"* our granddaughter exclaimed, proving yet again that we are inseparably connected to our gene pool, regardless of how our genes have expressed themselves from one generation to the next.

But how else do we accumulate the language we use? Sometimes I hear myself using words and phrases that sound just like those my brothers use. I'll occasionally catch a glimpse of myself in the mirror with a cap on and think, *Wow, I look just like you, Dad.* I'll also catch myself pulling on the skin under my neck just like my dad used to do. Or I'll find myself resting my hand in the same position my mom used to use. Even my fifty-something nephew, who is my dad's grandson, just confirmed that he also pulls on the skin of his neck just like the two previous generations.

Our inner voice is based on our experiences—all of them. The language we speak internally establishes what we think and what we say, whether positive or negative. As our inner language develops, we replay our language over and over again until we are convinced of who we think we are, and even how we think others perceive us, because that must be the truth, right?

It's important to know that the language of affirmation works both ways. On one hand, you can say, *I affirm that I'm a well-educated, fairly intelligent person with the ability to help others.* Or, on the other hand, you can say: *I affirm that no one likes me, because I'm not good-looking or smart.*

Which of those statements more closely resembles your inner life? Is it easy for you to positively affirm yourself, or is it easier to use negative affirmations? In reality, we give ourselves some kind of affirmation every day. What do you say to/about yourself on a daily basis? I've already said that we become what we believe is the truth. But is it really the truth?

Let's take a closer look at a positive change that has taken place in my life. I wish I could say this revelation from the Holy Spirit and the Scriptures came years ago. Unfortunately, I had no idea what was really bothering me. I had no way to identify it. Nor did I have the tools to change the way I thought. The man I wanted to be seemed completely out of reach, because I had believed all the lies from my youth.

Let me illustrate what I mean. As I was finishing my teaching degree, I was required to teach in a school setting for one college quarter. In my exit conference with my supervisor, she said I seemed insecure and unsure of myself. That comment not only stuck with me throughout the years, but it confirmed the negative feelings I had about my identity.

Years later, three years before retirement, we moved from a school district of about 700 students to a district of more than 20,000 students. It was the same kind of administrative job I'd held before, but on a much larger scale. I began this new position on August 5, and by November, it seemed wise to consider building a home, since I'd been commuting from my sister's home in a city nearby. Approaching my executive director, I asked, "Do you think it might be advisable to build a home in our new community?" He saw right through the question. "Leon, don't you know you're one of the most respected administrators in the building?" Of course, I hadn't known because I had no previous experience with positive reinforcement to help me accept success.

It took another ten years before I would begin to realize what was holding me back. In desperation, I called out to God. The Holy Spirit began to speak life into me through the Scriptures. Since then, I've experienced some major aha moments that literally changed my way of thinking.

For example, 1 Peter 4:10-11 taught me I have been given talents to serve and encourage others.

"God has given each of you a gift (talent) from his great variety of spiritual gifts. Use them well to serve one another. Do you have the gift of speaking? Then speak as though God himself were speaking through you. Do you have the gift of helping others? Do it with all the strength and energy that God supplies. Then everything you do will bring glory to God through Jesus Christ. All glory and power to him forever and ever! Amen."

It says "*each of you*"! No exceptions. God has given me a talent from His great variety of spiritual talents. But how would I be able to accept those talents if my negative inner messages held me back? I had to find a new language—new words to describe my inner talents and gifts. When I began to acknowledge my gifts from God as talents to serve others, an incredible thing happened. This process began to release those talents to a greater degree of service than ever before. While my skills and talents had been inferior in my mind, they were the talents God gave me, and I couldn't argue with that. Suddenly, it no longer mattered what anyone thought about my talents or how I was using them. All that mattered was that God was pleased when I used them to glorify Him. From that point on, I no longer allowed my former inner language to speak into my situation—ever. And I no longer worry whether someone is more talented than I. When that happens, I simply ask myself what I can learn from that person. And if my talents exceed those of others, I just make myself available to help them in any way I can.

In either situation, our Heavenly Father is glorified. I either grow my gifts by asking for help, or I use my skills and talents to teach or encourage others. Lots of people have asked me to help them in recent years. Had I not acknowledged my God-given gifts to the full extent God intended, then I wouldn't have been able to offer help. On the other hand, any time I believe I've learned all God can teach me, I lose my ability to glorify God due to my pride.

Remember, the Scripture teaches us to love our neighbor as we love ourselves? Well, loving ourselves first gives us the ability to love other people. Doing good deeds that glorify our Heavenly Father is a natural outgrowth of loving Jesus as our Savior. To serve others isn't burdensome at all because we do it out of love.

"Everyone who believes that Jesus is the Christ has become a child of God. And everyone who loves the Father loves his children, too. We know we love God's children if we love God and obey his commandments. Loving God means keeping his commandments, and his commandments are not burdensome. For every child of God defeats this evil world, and we achieve this victory through our faith. And who can win this battle against the world? Only those who believe that Jesus is the Son of God." (1 John 5:1-5)

Depending on your mindset, you might say, *But I'm not very spiritual, or I just don't know that much about the Bible.* Regardless of whether those statements are true, we all have to start somewhere, including me. What you're thinking is quite possibly just your old language speaking from your old voice.

You might already have a well-developed skill, e.g., repairing computers. How is that a spiritual gift from God? I believe everything in life can be attributed to God. Who created your aptitude for computer repair? How could your skill bring glory to our Heavenly Father? Imagine that the back of your business card has a Scripture verse that bears witness to your faith. The next person who picks up your business card has been deeply hurt emotionally and notices the Scripture. You sense this might be an opportunity to help, which opens the door for ministry to be led by the Holy Spirit. Had you not had the gift of computer repair, that person might have never found the service and thus the encouragement they needed. What if you donated your skills and talents (gifts) to someone in need or to your church? Again, our Heavenly Father would be glorified. Indeed, we can relate everything in life to the spiritual. When we practice our gifts, we are the beneficiaries of encouragement and blessing, and we see the faithfulness of the Holy Spirit to use our gifts.

Our inner messages aren't always the result of words. Could we create positive affirmations in these situations?

- when we feel appreciated by the nurturing touch of approval from others
- when someone gives us a compliment or a nod of approval
- when we receive an excellent performance review from a supervisor
- when you're convinced that your ability allows you to successfully accomplish things

Think of affirmations as something that can either tear down or build up. If people love God and themselves as demonstrated in the Scriptures, why would they speak with a negative inner voice as if God, our Creator, messed up? God never condemns us when we belong to Him. (John 8:1-11)

About three years ago, a friend offered to let me use his vacation home in a remote area. He described it as a place he goes to disconnect and unwind from daily responsibilities. This place had neither cell service nor internet access. He explained, "Just go and enjoy. Disconnect by having a quiet time to think with no one else to bother you." That meant I couldn't take my wife. I couldn't come down the mountain to make a cell call. I couldn't check my email or the news. I'd have no way to check on my business. In other words, it was an opportunity to look inside, to evaluate inner language and set goals. I couldn't imagine being unhooked for three weeks, so I declined his generous offer. Sometimes, I've wondered what might have been the outcome had I gone.

Imagine this same opportunity was offered to you, but changed in scope. In your mind's eye, you've just packed your bags for an extended trip to a foreign country where you don't speak the language. That's called immersion—the sink or swim method to learn the language of a foreign country. More new language develops the longer you are there. If you stay longer, your language evolves and eventually changes. Over time, you reach your goal to speak the language fluently. That's the way it is when we change the way we think. When we have rehearsed the new language based on how God sees us according to the Scriptures, we eventually become fluent in this new way of thinking.

What inner language do we develop as a result of trauma? Again, the inner words we speak can be either defeating or uplifting. God's either got this or He doesn't—and the answer is obviously that, yes, He's got whatever situations we face. It reminds me of the old hymn, The Solid Rock. There is a great affirmation waiting to be built. You can hear me play it at:

https://soundcloud.com/leon_johnson_piano/the-solid-rock

My hope is built on nothing less
than Jesus' blood and righteousness.
I dare not trust the sweetest frame,
but wholly lean on Jesus' name.
Chorus
On Christ, the solid Rock, I stand;
all other ground is sinking sand,
all other ground is sinking sand.

Have you ever watched a butcher prepare meat for the display case in a grocery store? Picture this. With a very sharp knife, the butcher cuts away the fat, leaving just enough marbling to produce a delicious, tender steak. The Scriptures are like that too. In fact, Hebrews 4:12 caused a major shift in my inner language. It wasn't that I didn't know these verses before. Years ago, I had even taught a course from the Book of Hebrews to a large adult group at church. Man, I loved those people. During my preparation for teaching each week's lesson, there were times when I could hardly type fast enough as the Holy Spirit gave insights I could never have seen on my own. Each week's delivery was a thrilling experience as I shared, asked pertinent questions, and encouraged people to think more deeply about what that Scripture meant. It wasn't as if I hadn't been made spiritually stronger by teaching, "For the word of God is alive and powerful." No disagreement there. "It is sharper than the sharpest two-edged sword." Again, no disagreement there. This next part was not fully realized, however: "Cutting between soul and spirit, between joint and marrow." That portion of Scripture was particularly troubling to me. I had difficulty understanding the meaning. In reality, I realized that it exposes our innermost thoughts and desires. That was it, my lightbulb moment. There were plenty of innermost thoughts and desires which, had I been honest with myself, would have been a gauge for how committed I had been both to loving myself and others, as well as relinquishing my old ways of thinking. It wasn't that I didn't want to confess Christ. It wasn't even that I didn't want to be a good Christian. When I asked God to heal me of my innermost thoughts and desires, life started to become so much clearer. The difference was in allowing the words into my spirit to cut away old thinking.

When I started praying, "Search me, O God, and know my heart," I felt exposed and vulnerable. The next phrase, "Test me and know my anxious thoughts" ...I'd had plenty of experience with that. Imagine admitting that God knows all my thoughts, both righteous and unrighteous.

This prayer contains two more questions to address—first, "See if there is any offensive way in me." I was giving the Holy Spirit permission to reveal any area of my life that didn't please God. Again, it's a vulnerable place to be since there is never just one area. It's like living in a ten-room house. The last room has finally been cleaned just in time to start over from the beginning. Believe me, I'm not looking for a sin behind every piece of furniture or potted plant, but it seems the Holy Spirit is never finished revealing who I am. Life situations come and go. These situations result in victory and wisdom and sometimes a need to ask forgiveness.

To me, the last question is the most important part of the prayer— "and lead me in the way everlasting." My desire to yield to God's ways will clean up my inner heart. When I live according to the Spirit (Galatians 5:25), that gives life. A yielded, humble spirit will be ready to encourage others. (James 4:6)

My innermost thoughts and desires were not healthy. But as the Holy Spirit exposed my old way of thinking, the process of changing who I was to who I am today began. My life experiences have taught me that God does His best work when we are at the point of desperation. Day by day, the Scriptures strengthened my resolve to be who God planned for me to be. "But in my distress, I cried out to the LORD; yes, I prayed to my God for help. He heard me from his sanctuary; my cry to him reached his ears" (Psalm 18:6).

Because we're all individuals, God, through the impressions and expressions of the Holy Spirit, refines who we are in different ways. I feel strongly, however, that the Scriptures will play a large role in the process of change, regardless of a person's circumstances.

Try as I might, I couldn't help but struggle with algebra in high school, because it was a language I didn't understand. It seemed like no other math language I'd ever heard. That's the way it was with some key Scriptures like Romans 12:1-2, which said we were to present our bodies as a living sacrifice, and do so by the renewing of our minds. All of that was like a foreign language to me. During the beginning stages of my changed life, I read the passage from another translation, the New Living Translation (NLT). It was as if I could all of a sudden do spiritual algebra, if there were such a thing. How do you think this applies?

And so, dear brothers and sisters, I plead with you to give your bodies to God because of all he has done for you. Let them be a living and holy sacrifice—the kind he will find acceptable. This is truly the way to worship him. Don't copy the behavior and customs of this world, but let God transform you into a new person by changing the way you think. Then you will learn to know God's will for you, which is good and pleasing and perfect. (Romans 12:1-2)

Now, that was and is attainable. God gave us the ability to control our thoughts. I'll just love God and change the way I think. And just like that, the transition began, and my thoughts became His thoughts. I had finally yielded my spirit to God's Spirit. This yielding is not a one-time thing, but a daily occurrence. It didn't happen overnight, but the way is now clear. I can meet negative thoughts with the truth of Scripture. Refuting the personal lies I'd been telling myself since I was in primary school reminds me of what Neil Anderson[2], author of The Bondage Breaker said: "You don't have to outshout him (Satan) or outmuscle him to be free of his influence. You just have to *out truth Him*. Believe, declare, and act upon the truth of God's Word, and you will thwart Satan's strategy."

Robert Morris[3], pastor of Gateway Church in Southlake, Texas, is a respected worldwide speaker. My wife and I have had the distinct pleasure of listening to him speak at conferences, on television and online. He is a great example of a person who hears and knows the impressions of the Holy Spirit. His God-given gift of insight pierces the Scriptures, giving us an even deeper understanding in both context and truth. Here's how Pastor Morris explained Romans 12:1-2: *Renewing your mind—that is, replacing falsehood and deception with spiritual truth—changes you from the inside out. It will absolutely transform every area of your life. You do this by letting God speak to you! (And believing what He says, of course!)*

And that's exactly what we're talking about here. Once I began doing that, I knew the change in thought was underway. The truth of Ephesians 2:10 was absolutely life-changing for me: For we are God's masterpiece. He has created us anew in Christ Jesus, so we can do the good things he planned for us long ago." Another translation says, "For we are God's workmanship." Think of it this way: The God of our creation made us His masterpieces (God's workmanship) with the good things He long ago planned for us to do. When considering the workmanship of a product, we wouldn't purchase it if it didn't live up to the advertised capabilities. Have you ever purchased a highly-rated product that wasn't able to do the job? Fortunately, with God as our Maker, we never have to worry about not being able to do what God planned for us long ago; He has built within us the talents (gifts) and qualities necessary to carry out the plans He has for us, though we can always practice and enhance our gifts throughout life. The more we practice our gifts, the more skilled we become at using them for ministry and for life, especially when the Holy Spirit is our Helper. (See 1 Peter 4:10-11, Romans 12:6-8, Ephesians 4:12-13, and 2 Peter 1:3.)

Once we begin this process of change, we may find that we tend to experience a momentary relapse in our inner life. That's actually not uncommon. If you were living in that foreign country we mentioned earlier, you might sometimes wish you could just answer in your native language—it's easier. In the same way, it's hard to change the inner language we've believed about how we perceive ourselves. But once we become keenly aware of that language, we must stay the course to learn the way of the Scriptures.

As I transitioned to my new Scriptural way of thinking, it was very important for me to repent and ask forgiveness. You might be thinking, Wait. What did I do wrong? Why is forgiveness necessary? According to Scripture, repentance means to turn around and go the other way when we get off track. This principle will become clear as you pray the prayer at the end of this chapter. As you pray, you can also ask the Holy Spirit to make you more aware of your inner language, as already referenced in Chapter 1 in John 14:26-27.

The Scriptures have the answer for speaking life in this new way of thinking. Philippians 4:6-9 teaches me to not "worry about anything; instead, pray about everything. Tell God what you need, and thank him for all he has done. Then you will experience God's peace, which exceeds anything we can understand. His peace will guard your hearts and minds as you live in Christ Jesus. And now, dear brothers and sisters, one final thing. Fix your thoughts on what is true, and honorable, and right, and pure, and lovely, and admirable. Think about things that are excellent and worthy of praise. Keep putting into practice all you learned and received from me—everything you heard from me and saw me doing. Then the God of peace will be with you."

Our negative inner thoughts do not come from our Heavenly Father by way of the Holy Spirit. Satan is the accuser. In our natural sin nature, we might be reminded by the Holy Spirit of an area in our life that needs to change, but God never tears us down with guilt or negative thoughts that devalue us. That's against His nature.

Intervarsity is a well-known national campus ministry. This organization defines spiritual warfare as *the leveraging of everything that God promises against everything that opposes God's purposes*[4]. If there was not such a thing as spiritual warfare, we would always have smooth sailing in life—no more negative thoughts, no more temptations to make sinful decisions because of our own selfishness, and no more evil in the world. Thankfully, since we do have to engage in spiritual warfare, Scripture contains protection for that battle. "We are human, but we don't wage war as humans do. We use God's mighty weapons, not worldly weapons, to knock down the strongholds of human reasoning and to destroy false arguments. We destroy every proud obstacle that keeps people from knowing God. We capture their rebellious thoughts and teach them to obey Christ" (2 Corinthians 10:3-5).

In other words, we don't fight with our fists in some kind of physical battle. We fight in the spiritual realm, and we have spiritual weapons at our disposal. The weapons we use will depend on the situation we're facing—including praying and interceding in the Spirit (Galatians 5:25, Romans 8:34), reading and meditating on the Scriptures, fasting, rebuking Satan and his demons in Jesus' name, and joining with others to stand against a stronghold. A stronghold is something that holds someone back from doing the right thing. My stronghold included repeating negative inner messages. As we steep ourselves in the truth of God's Word, we begin to break our stronghold by changing the way we think and speak. We can break all kinds of strongholds by removing the obstacles that cause them. My negative messages were preventing me from living a life of peace, but that obstacle was removed by applying the truth revealed in Romans 12:1-2.

I've recently realized that the deciding factor is the presence or absence of a sincere desire to break a stronghold. During the Covid-19 pandemic and the required stay-at-home order in our state, I've had this extra side relationship with our refrigerator. The refrigerator itself wasn't the obstacle, but what's in the refrigerator was an issue. Or was the problem the way I think about what's in that fridge? As long as I'm being vulnerable, the pantry has always been a problem—by that, I mean what is in the pantry, right? Those are two obstacles that I have yet to determine whether I want to remove. Since we can't get rid of the refrigerator—talk about being essential—the obstacles have more to do with my mind than what is in the refrigerator. The pantry has to be looked at separately. It's just the way I think. A pantry seems pretty essential to our home's function and design. It's filled with really good, nutritious foods. But one shelf in the pantry, in my opinion, has a snack basket containing what I consider non-essential items. It's also stuffed full of good-tasting foods of lesser nutritious value—my wife and I call those "fun foods." Clearly, there are choices to be made here. Which of these four is the true obstacle? The essential refrigerator? The mostly essential pantry? The fun food in the snack basket? Or my mind? Of course, it's my mind that seems to be the obstacle. Do I need to apply the principle found in Romans 12:2 all over again and change the way I think? Do I want to change the way I think about food or don't I? Is changing the way I think about food going to apply to other areas of my life? Am I willing to let it?

This stronghold with food impacts every decision I make about food. There are days I'm in control of the stronghold and others when I have no intention of removing the obstacle to any kind of food. I just don't want to. When that happens, I rationalize that I deserve it. It entertains. It satisfies. It betrays.

I'm sure my wife breathed a sigh of relief when she began reading the previous paragraph. She probably initially thought I was going to ask her to get rid of the non-essential snack basket just because I can't control myself around it. Those who know my wife know exactly what I mean, and I'll bet some of you readers think the snack basket should be gone too! It's non-essential. Why put temptation in my way? That snack basket has a reserved spot in the pantry, third shelf down, just to the right of center. It's a great location—easy access to the fun food it contains. We could really substitute any stronghold for that snack basket, then go through the process of determining the obstacles in the way of overcoming the stronghold or whether we even want to deal with it.

Notice how I used the phrase "reserved spot" in describing the location of our snacks? When it comes to our internal temptations, we have a similar reserved spot in our inner being that's off limits. It's hidden under lock and key until we're vulnerable enough to allow the Holy Spirit to change us. Until that time, it remains a separate room, locked away from the Lord's influence. The mind is unwilling to yield the key, preventing that reserved spot from being opened up and cleaned. Sometimes, even when that last room in our heart is unlocked for cleaning, it's hard to get at the grit in the corners, those last remnants we continue to hold in reserve from the Holy Spirit's ministry to our soul. Mine is that third shelf down just to the right of center. Hands off!

How in the world could I have written so personally about my own struggle? And, how does my personal stronghold relate to this chapter about negative inner self talk? Let me illustrate.

- I know I have a problem with food which has become somewhat of an idol, but have you seen the way that older guy eats at church potlucks? He has a much bigger problem than I do.
- At the grocery store last week, a family was shopping with a huge, overloaded cart seemingly filled with mostly fun foods. These people were heavy too—I mean really big people. It goes without saying that their snack basket at home has to be much larger than ours. Besides, I don't think I even have a problem at all compared to them.
- I realize I have one remaining corner deep down in my heart where I'm still wrestling with a little grit. But the entire upstairs of my boss's heart has all kinds of stuff in different rooms. He thinks it's hidden, but I know because he talks about how he lives. He's got problems far deeper than mine. I'm not so bad after all.

Comparison is everywhere. Thanks for talking through that with me.

"It's too hard to change," someone once said to me. It seems odd that the pain of changing would be greater than the pain of a negative, self-deprecating life. Another person said, "I don't think I'm willing to spend time reading the Scriptures the way you do." We make time for what is important to us. It's probably the norm for people to sit down to two or three meals every day. What if it were the norm to sit down with the Scriptures for fifteen minutes each day? Food left on our plates will not be applied to our body. Scriptures left in the Book or unread on some digital device will not be applied to our spiritual body either.

When the pain of my insecurity became very great, I cried out to God for help—for answers to find the root of these insecurities. The answers were in the Scriptures. Now that I've discovered them, I'm at peace with God and my inner being. Letting the Scriptures be absorbed into my spirit allowed the truth of Romans 8:6 to become a part of me. "So, letting your sinful nature control your mind leads to (spiritual) death. But letting the Spirit control your mind leads to life and peace."

Though I'm not a certified counselor, people have sought my counsel, especially in the last five years. It's difficult to explain why this happens, but people seem to be drawn to my spirit. Our paths will cross at church or somewhere else, and they'll ask to meet with me. Sometimes, I won't even know them, yet they will want to connect with me through social media. We're not long into a face-to-face conversation before people are pouring out their hearts to me. It's an amazing and spectacular thing when you realize the divine appointment taking place, orchestrated by the Holy Spirit.

One such event took place a few months ago when an unexpected phone call came from Jake, who's married to an alcoholic. She had left home to be with her husband's good friend, to do some binge drinking. Evening turned to night, and night to morning, and she still hadn't come home. Jake was distraught by what was happening, especially when he realized where his wife was. He became so angry that he jumped in his car to drive to his friend's home to "have it out" with someone who perhaps wasn't going to be his friend much longer. By asserting himself into this situation in a very unhealthy way, he was about to blow up his life and his marriage. But on the way, the Holy Spirit impressed his heart, saying, "pull over and stop the car. Call Leon."

"Can I come over?" he asked. I asked him when he wanted to meet with me. "Now!" Jake was crying and seemed desperate to find answers as he explained what had happened over the phone. He arrived within a few minutes and broke down, pouring out his story from a broken heart.

I was praying in the Spirit about what to say that would bring him down from his agitated state to some level of peace. Remember that Scripture from Hebrews 4:12 about the Scriptures being sharper than any two-edged sword? The Scriptures began to flow in the most organized way, many of which I'm sharing with you in this chapter. The counsel of the Holy Spirit was undeniable as He began to cut through the confusion for Jake. He asked for paper and pen and wrote down every single Scripture reference as I shared them. We prayed together. At that point, Jake was calm and at peace—no longer agitated. When he was ready to leave, he told me, "I learned more in this meeting together than I've ever learned about God before."

Now, I could have taken all the credit for the success of that meeting with Jake, but if I had, that would have been the beginning of the end of my ministry to others. Jake's situation later resolved in a peaceful way. The next day, there was a photo of the hand-written paper of all those Scripture references posted to social media. The caption on the post explained how he had found a new way of thinking. Though our life's battles may rage on, we can still remain at peace when we focus on the message of the Scriptures. Jake was convinced by the power of the Scriptures of a much better way to live.

Jake's story has a postscript. Just last week, another crisis occurred with his wife. She had been clean of alcohol for three months, but had apparently ordered a substance online which caused her to go into serious seizures. After several days of observation in a hospital, she became so agitated that they transferred her to the psych ward. He was unable to see her because of the privacy laws in our state. He had no rights and faced another traumatic emotional struggle. How would he respond? Would he hold onto the Scriptures that changed his perspective and restored his peace? Or would he fall apart, reverting back to his old mindset? I'm thrilled to report that he held on to his new perspective, remaining at peace in the midst of the trial. He hung on to the peace he discovered in Romans 12:18, which commands, "Do all that you can to live in peace with everyone."

We've covered a lot of ground in Chapter 2. Separating the principle of the light of God from the spiritual darkness of this world sets us on the path to peace. "This is the message we heard from Jesus and now declare to you: God is light, and there is no darkness in him at all" (1 John 1:5).

IMMUTABLE PRINCIPLE #3: I will stop any negative self-talk and surrender to a new, more positive way of thinking about how God perceives me. The truth of Scripture will help contradict negative self-talk. I will meditate on these Scriptures again and again until the lies are extinguished. My new desire and commitment to change is possible by experiencing God in a new, deeper way. I will ask God to show me any strongholds in my life that need to be identified and released with the help of the Holy Spirit so my spirit can be free.

"Blessed are they which do hunger and thirst after righteousness: for they shall be filled" (Matthew 5:6, KJV).

PRAYER: "Father, in Jesus' holy name, I ask You to forgive me for thinking I'm less than I am. I have believed the negative inner lies that have been repeatedly whispered and entertained in my spirit. Help me to focus on the language You taught me through the Scriptures about who I am. Thank You for forgiving me. Amen."

There is even more hope ahead. Hint: Caught in the net.

At the end of each chapter, watch for the immutable (unchangeable) principle that I adopted that led him to a place of peace for my inner man.

CHAPTER 3

CAUGHT IN THE NET

Insecurities & Comparison

Depending on our life experiences, we probably all have an image that comes to mind when we think of the word "net." Maybe you thought about the internet or a fishnet or the mesh net of a trampoline. There's even a mesh router system now that is supposed to improve wireless signal strength for connecting to the web. Chefs might wear a hairnet while they're cooking to keep hair from falling into the food they're preparing. Regardless of the image you have in mind, one thing is certain. Nets generally have just one purpose, and that is to trap something.

I was twelve years old when I went with my boys' Sunday school class on an all-night camping trip. Our teacher took us to a beautiful area called Salmon la Sac near Roslyn, Washington. After breakfast the next morning, we packed up all our gear and started hiking down the narrow, forested trail back out to the car. One boy held a fishing net over his shoulder, and within that net were some camping supplies that were obviously too heavy for the net. With every step he took, the net bounced under the weight, causing the frame to weaken. Finally, the lightweight aluminum handle broke into two pieces right at the net's rounded frame, and the net's contents clattered to the ground with a noisy thud.

The truth of the matter is that nets are usually pretty secure pieces of equipment. It's difficult to break free from a well-designed net. Put enough pressure on a net, however, and we're likely lose something...a fish or a strand of hair or—perish the thought—a trapeze artist.

Practically speaking, the entire human race has the kind of net I'm talking about…it's the comparison net. Think about this: My inner voice would often create a response based on who or what I compared myself to. Whenever I make a comparison, I immediately make a judgment. It could be something as simple as where to buy gas, or the best method to solve a problem, or heaven forbid, a judgment about who I am. Am I this or am I that? Have I measured up in my comparison or do I feel inadequate? Are my skills and talents equal to or greater than those of someone else? Am I comfortable fitting in with a certain group? Comparison starts in the morning when I get up and ends when I fall asleep. Most of the time, I'm not even aware I'm doing it. The kinds of comparison I allow always has a result—either a positive or a negative affirmation as described in Chapter 2. And those negative affirmations always end up putting so much pressure on the comparison net that we end up losing something very important.

A good friend I'll call Ann said that between the ages of six and eight she began to compare herself to both her older and younger sisters. I believe her story demonstrates the perfect storm regarding the issue of comparison:

"My older sister was very talented—musically, artistically, rhythmically. She was a blonde-haired, blue-eyed girl with dimples and an outgoing personality. Though only fourteen months older than me, she was more like a mother than a sister to me.

My younger sister was five years younger and also beautiful. Her blue eyes, dimples, and straight hair seemed to motivate my mother's friends to give her gifts. I, however, was the brown-eyed one with super curly hair—the short, very shy, and untalented sister. Both my sisters had many fun friends, while I was the loner, the wallflower.

For a long time, I just never fit into the emotionally maturing group. Several circumstances forced me to take charge of my life to build the confidence I needed. Though I'm still shy, I've learned I must step up to what God is calling me to do.

It didn't help that my parents were struggling with their own issues. To add to the dysfunction, my younger sister became the black sheep of the family, causing my parents to devote far more time to her. Other traumas caused me to examine my relationship with the Lord. Who really was this God I thought I knew, and what did I really know about Him? As I encountered and discovered more of God through the Scriptures, a new and beautiful nearness and expression of love, knowledge and wisdom began to change me. It's been like the song, "In the Garden." I am His, and He is mine...FOREVER. I am molded together by the blood of Jesus Christ. I know that I know. My feet follow the Savior's. He gave His life on the cross for me. I am God's creation and have been given His love, mercy and saving grace. I am who He says I am."

Thanks for sharing your personal story, Ann.

I hope you took note of Ann's inner language. This is the time to discover how comparison affects our inner language. First, it's really hard to stop comparing, because we've been doing it forever. We just never stop to think about whether it's causing us to tear ourselves down or build ourselves up. Have you ever thought about how comparison can build us up? For example, you see a person or group of people in formal attire enjoying conversation and laughter at their event. What does your inner voice say?

- Wow, those people are having a great time. Wonder what event they're attending? It's cool they are such good friends.
- Look at how well dressed they are. Bet they get together for a group picture before they call it a night.
- Everyone looks so happy with their friends. I don't have friends like that.
- I remember dressing up like that for a party last month. The people I was with complimented me on how I looked.
- That guy who seemingly was the life of the party kept people laughing. I could never be like him.

In any scenario you have imagined or experienced, can you relate to any of these *contrasting statements*?

- I could never be as good as them *OR* I wonder what I could learn from them?
- At least I finished college *OR* I am grateful for my education.
- If I could have a career like theirs, I could be more successful OR What are some ways (without comparing to others) I could enhance my career that would benefit my family?
- They act like they're better than I *OR* The Scriptures say that God does not show favoritism.
- Their relationships appear better than most of mine *OR* I can see now how I've chosen my friends because they're important to my spiritual health and sense of belonging.
- Their children are better behaved than mine *OR* I really admire their parenting skills. I'll ask some questions about their philosophy of childrearing to learn why it seems to work so well.
- Their clothes and the cars they drive always trip triggers about my own inadequacies and career *OR* As a car guy, it's always fun to look at cars. It would be great to know what they like and dislike about them compared to what I've read. I'd like to get to know them better anyway.
- Only beautiful people are in the movies. I could never be an actor *OR* According to Scripture, we all have God-given talents. Since I've lived out what God planned for me, I've been enough since the beginning.
- My friends' social media triggers me every single day. It always causes me to think my life is in a very tough place. I am depressed by what others have posted about their perfect lives. My life isn't perfect even though I try to make my posts look like I'm living a great life *OR* I realize everyone has strengths and weaknesses. It makes me ask myself if social media is building me up or tearing me down. Maybe I'll take a break from social media for a while.

Many more possible comparisons exist, but you get my point. Those secondary statements may seem too challenging to accomplish or even consider. I've had to learn to ask myself, "What is my true state of being, and what is the one true godly course set before me?" Those secondary statements used to seem unrealistic because my thought life wouldn't allow it. They were wholly unfamiliar. But the more I meditated on Scriptural truths, the more the thoughts became my own.

We are intensely focused on ourselves, often making assessments of how we measure up. Do we compare our clothing to current fashion or to another person? Comparison shopping is essential. Nothing wrong with that unless it triggers the wrong kinds of reactions inside us. Have you compared your neighbor's yard to yours, given yourself a negative or positive affirmation, or hired a landscaper as a result of comparison?

Comparing those within our family unit is always a challenge. Jockeying for position and power has been inevitable since the Garden of Eden where Cain killed Abel out of jealousy. A great divide occurred in Isaac and Rebekah's family when Esau lost his birthright to his twin brother, Jacob. The whisper of Satan's impressions on my inner life used to be enough to start the wheels of comparison turning.

Sometimes, even without realizing it, I allowed him to set his evil trap.

For a period of time, I wasn't sure how my wife felt about me anymore. Satan took a smattering of truth about how busy she was, and started feeding me half-truths out of context. The evil one kept at it until he'd made a pretty good case. I believed the lies I'd built up in my head, even though they weren't true. Satan tried to divide us while I tried to rationalize why I had every reason to feel as I did. But now, I see the incredible patience and persistence Satan uses to lead a person along until the trap has been set. Thank God, my wife was able to dispel his lies, and Satan lost that battle.

Nowadays, I confront Satan with the facts of Scripture or by asking questions in a discussion with someone without accusing, or by praying and seeking wisdom from God. That's how the power of the Holy Spirit is evident in my life—actively reading and meditating on the Scriptures and listening for the Holy Spirit to respond. Living like this has brought unshakable peace to my soul. The truth is that I've never felt so comfortable with who I am.

Jesus said in John 10:27-30, "My sheep listen to my voice; I know them, and they follow me." Jesus knows me. He loves me. I have a reason to listen. "I give them eternal life, and they will never perish." Eternal life is not in question. I will live eternally. "No one can snatch them away from me, for my Father has given them to me" Being in Christ makes me secure in this life and the life to come… "and he is more powerful than anyone else. No one can snatch them from the Father's hand. The Father and I are one." The more I experience God in my spirit, the more I can experience the oneness Jesus Himself promised me in His Word.

It's difficult to free us from the comparison trap. Comparing ourselves to others becomes a habitual entanglement that entices us to believe things about ourselves that don't agree with Scripture. Has all of the personal comparison over my lifespan helped me to feel better? Did it make a difference in my quality of life? Did those comparisons add to my value in any way? Asking those questions enabled me to realize I didn't need to prove my value to anyone. All I had to do was love God and serve Him only. (Luke 4:8) God showed me He has no favorites. (Romans 2:10-11)

Did you know James was the half-brother of Jesus? Three different men were named James in the early church, so to distinguish the three, Jesus' half-brother was named James the Less. Now, I don't know if they actually called him *The Less* as part of his name, but imagine how he must have felt if they did. If anyone had a right to be in bondage to comparison, it was James. His half-brother was that amazing guy known as Jesus who knew no sin—perfect in every way.

James could never measure up to Jesus. Comparison would have been crippling for James given their mutual lineage. In the same way, it can be crippling to us, too.

James finally understood the truth of who Jesus was. After all, he wrote the Epistle of James, a sharply-worded book that has the potential to make us all feel pretty uncomfortable if we struggle in the areas of our humanness that James covers. James asked, "What good is it, dear brothers and sisters, if you say you have faith but don't show it by your actions? So, you see, faith by itself isn't enough. Unless it produces good deeds, it is dead and useless." Though I had lived a consistent life of service in the church to encourage others, because of this passage, I was now motivated by a newfound passion for it, both inside and outside the church building.

The less I compared myself to others, the more I discovered faith had a purpose. Author Bob Goff[7] captured a perfect definition for comparison: *"We won't be distracted by comparison if we are captivated by purpose."* Captivated is a very powerful descriptor. I'm not even at the end of the chapter yet, and I've already shared the solution for a life stuck in comparison—apply purpose. Jesus had eternal purpose. We have a similar purpose if we choose to accept it.

Rick Warren, pastor of Saddleback Church, wrote a New York Times best-selling book, The Purpose Driven Life—What on Earth Am I Here For? This book has dramatically changed the lives of many people. If purpose were not an important component of a peaceful life, there wouldn't be so much written about it. I highly recommend always choosing Bible-based resources about purpose to maintain an accurate perspective on living the Christian life.

The Scriptures prove who we are. Consider how Jenn's life changed after she read about how God loved her from the beginning:

My whole life has been a life of comparison, and it left me with the feeling that I would never be as good as anyone else. It started early in my childhood when I felt like I didn't fit in and often compared myself to others. I was raised by a single alcoholic mother and a father that I saw maybe a handful of times. My mother would go on a drinking bender for several days at a time, and sometimes even weeks. She would always come back and act like nothing ever happened. You see, my mother couldn't metabolize alcohol very well and even small amounts would leave her wasted.

On one occasion, my grandparents asked my mother where I was, and sadly she couldn't remember. From that point on, they decided that she could drop me off with them at any time, no questions asked. After that, I routinely exited the school bus on Fridays and arrived home to find my mother drinking. I would immediately know to go pack my bags as I would be going to my grandparents' house. I was embarrassed as I wondered how many of the kids would notice.

My mother didn't work a traditional job very often due to mental illnesses that interfered with the stability a job requires. The main source of income throughout my entire childhood was a welfare check. However, when she was sober, she was a good mom. She would make dinner every night, the house was clean, the yard was taken care of, and there was often a baked treat after school. During that time, I compared myself to my peers who had typical families. I asked myself: "Why do I stay with my grandparents so often? None of my friends do that. Why are we poor? Why don't I have a dad—everyone at school made Father's Day gifts.

The destructive negative self-talk even turned into comparisons about beauty, intellectual abilities, and body image. Those comparisons hung over my head like a black cloud that would negatively affect every area of my life for many years to come, making me resentful even into my early twenties. I spent years torturing myself, yet all it took was one chapter in a book to set me free. I was no longer bound by negative thoughts and comparisons. I was able to start accepting myself and forgive my mother. The book was The Purpose Driven Life by Rick Warren[5].

Long before you were conceived by your parents, you were conceived in the mind of God.

Most amazing, God decided how you would be born. Regardless of the circumstances of your birth or who your parents are, God had a plan in creating you. It doesn't matter whether your parents were good, bad, or indifferent. God knew that those two individuals possessed exactly the right genetic makeup to create the customer "you" he had in mind. They had the DNA God wanted to make you.

While there are illegitimate parents, there are no illegitimate children. Many children are unplanned by their parents, but they are not unplanned by God. God's purpose took into account human error, and even sin.

God never does anything accidently, and he never makes mistakes. He has a reason for everything he creates. Every plant and every animal were planned by God, and every person was designed with a purpose in mind.

It's that simple...God chose me and He loves me unconditionally.

Ephesians 1:4 gave me the evidence I needed to believe: "Even before he made the world, God loved us and chose us in Christ to be holy and without fault in his eyes." Then 1 John 3:1 helped me to understand the depths of God's love. "See how very much our Father loves us, for he calls us his children, and that is what we are! But the people who belong to this world don't recognize that we are God's children because they don't know him."

Jenn, thanks for sharing your personal story.

I've known Jenn practically her whole life. In recent years, it was such a blessing to learn she had received Jesus as her Savior, and to be able to encourage her from time to time as the Holy Spirit directed.

Nearly every day God uses my God-given skills and talents in big and small ways to encourage others. It's extremely rewarding to help others as Jesus taught in Scripture. In the process, I had to take my focus off myself and place it on God in a much more meaningful way. When we are in relationship with the Son of God, we can discover His divine purpose.

A phenomenal thing happened in 2019 when we attended a major international convention in Orlando, Florida. We'd gone to the evening worship service where there were an estimated 7,000 people. I had no sooner sat down beside a millennial guy I'd never met, when I felt in my spirit that I would talk to him at the end of the service about his life's purpose. Then at the end of the sermon, the congregation was asked to join hands in small groups and ask how we could pray for each other. When I asked this guy how we could pray for him, he replied, "Pray about life's purpose for me." I leaned over and told him I had known from the moment I sat down that I was supposed to talk with him about that very thing. Then we briefly prayed together, and I shared four Scriptures about God's purpose for each of us, and how He's not only known us from the beginning, but also thinks about us all the time. He thanked me for the confirmation and asked me to remember him in prayer in the days ahead. As we continued to talk, I also learned he knew our former pastor from years earlier in Washington state. If you're a believer, I encourage you to follow the lead of the Holy Spirit in encouraging others.

This checklist may be of help to hone your purpose:
- Be involved in a good Bible-believing church where you can help others and learn more and more about Jesus through the Scriptures. Find a place to serve at your church, whether directly with people or behind the scenes if that's where you feel more comfortable. Attending is not the same as being involved in ministry.
- Be a humble and willing example of a servant. Jesus said He came to serve and be a ransom for many.
- Read the Scriptures every day, not because we have to, but out of love for the Savior.
- Practice listening to the subtle impressions of the Holy Spirit.
- Share the Scriptures you're reading or studying with others.
- Doing so...

- o encourages them.
- o helps you to remember the Scriptures for your own benefit.
- o helps you to hear what the Holy Spirit may be teaching you as you dwell in the Word.
- o encourages you in your faith when you realize sharing may provide opportunities for divine appointments.

- Spend time in private prayer, especially before you read the Scriptures. Doing so will help to quiet your spirit before reading. You will also be more likely to feel God's presence or hear impressions from the Holy Spirit.

- Always be ready to tell your story about how Jesus has helped or changed you. It's far more powerful than you can imagine. As you share your story, it may potentially remind you of other life stories; but don't compare your Jesus story to the stories of others. Use others' stories to encourage you in the faith.

- Allow people with whom you come in contact to share their own stories or difficulties. Be a good listener. When I'm trying to help others, I sometimes have no idea how to address their issues. People talk to me about finances, relationship and marriage problems, spiritual issues and marital faithfulness, employment or retirement issues—the topics are varied. If that's the case with you, don't let it prevent you from listening carefully. I readily listen to the Holy Spirit for Scriptures that might come to mind that may be of help. If I think of a possible solution, I offer it. But when I don't know how to help, I'll let them know that as well. At times I might say something like, 'It might be helpful for you to speak with your pastor, a counselor or someone who has expertise in that area.' Over the years, God has given me many divine appointments to encourage others. In fact, Scripture says we have an obligation to comfort those who need to be comforted. Allowing people the opportunity to talk through their problems may lead them to discover their own solutions. The power of speaking the words out loud may give them clarity. Sometimes asking clarifying questions also helps people to arrive at a solution.

This practical checklist is just a part of everyday life. Don't try to make it happen—just let it happen. Let these things become a way of life. As life unfolds each day, let purpose unfold naturally, and be ready to carry out the lessons of the Scriptures. I am always amazed at how a yielded life can be a bright beacon for others.

A friend I've known for perhaps forty years had consented to be a reader for the first three chapters of my manuscript to provide feedback. As I was busy writing, she messaged saying she had been at the hospital emergency room three times in recent days because the vision in her eye had deteriorated, causing severe pain. Without thinking, I immediately prayed over her message and then texted back: "In Jesus' holy and powerful name, I ask that You restore Emma's vision for she is Your servant. You withhold no good thing from Your children. We believe You are in the business of restoration. We agree together this will improve and resolve according to Your will. Amen." That same evening, she followed up with a text saying,

"My vision has cleared up! Thank you, Jesus!"

When I started my day, I hadn't planned to speak with Emma, but I was suddenly compelled to connect with her. During our conversation, she agreed to read some Scriptures I sent, but then she went on to describe her current struggle with reading. This is a perfect example of letting life happen. The communication wasn't planned, yet the ministry of the Holy Spirit was at work. Joining together in prayer, we glorified the Lord by our obedience to stand in faith for her healing. The truth is that it takes practice to obey the leading of the Holy Spirit. Yet, every time we obey, it builds our faith and increases our boldness, because we know we can trust Him. And, of course, it allows us to encourage others.

Remember when I mentioned the difference between knowing about God and letting God reach our emotions so that we remember who we are? The natural outgrowth of knowing our identity in God is to know we were born for a purpose. To that end, we're motivated to share our faith stories and encourage others, and that's exactly why I'm sharing these stories. Just as Jesus' story is one of hope and peace that blesses others, our stories are proof that we want to serve Him because we love Him. Now, before you think you just have to try harder to be a Christian, consider this. If you've ever been in a loving relationship with another human being, your love for that person is unconditional.

- You do things for them without being asked.
- You try to please them.
- You authentically affirm them.
- You express your thanks to them, because they mean so much to you.

Loving Jesus is like having a loving relationship with your mate. He desires our worship, trust, loyalty, relationship and service. It's easy to give those things because we're in relationship with him. Getting off track in our relationship with Jesus leaves us feeling vulnerable and insecure. People may exchange the joy they once had as a believer in Christ for what the world has to offer, but that kind of joy is only temporary.

As early as 1670, Blaise Pascal[6], a seventeenth- century French philosopher, in a defense of the Christian faith, Pensées, wrote that every human being has a place inside that needs to be filled:

"What else does this craving and this helplessness proclaim but that there was once in man a true happiness, of which all that now remains is the empty print and trace? This he tries in vain to fill with everything around him, seeking in things that are not there the help he cannot find in those that are, though none can help, since this infinite abyss can be filled only with an infinite and immutable object; in other words, by God himself."

Several others have since written about a "God-shaped hole." Without the authentic joy that comes from being a Christ follower, how can we possibly fill those God-shaped holes? The world has many to offer. Unfortunately, all joy substitutes are temporary and require an escalating and endless supply of the chosen substitute. People will always search for a medication of choice to finally fill their spiritual need, but that hole will not be filled until they find or return to Jesus as Savior. That brings us back full circle, to a life of meaningful purpose.

When I catch myself making comparisons to others, and I do sometimes, it's usually because they've tripped some kind of trigger from my past that reminds me of my old sense of inadequacy. It could be as innocent as seeing people enjoying their youth, grieving for a moment that my youth has passed, and then confessing in a short prayer that my dependence is on God, not on my youth.

In the process of letting God change me, I had to choose not to give up my pursuit of God. From the outset, I pursued God. I am pursuing God. I will continue to pursue God. I pursue God in prayer, in the Scriptures and in service to others. Does that sound difficult to do? Not one bit, because I have purpose. It's important to remember that the world is full of distractions that try to keep our focus off target, that try to keep us focused on situations and struggles rather than our purpose. When we know why we're here and focus on that, nothing can empty our emotional bucket ever again. That's why I am determined to not lose my focus on my purpose. I can't allow myself to "love this world nor the things it offers" me. Self-sabotage is real and happens when we focus on the wrong things, "for when I love the world, I do not have the love of the Father in me" (1 John 2:15).

A return to my old way of thinking would not only be disastrous to my way of life as a Christ follower, but it would also hinder my ability to hear the prompting of the Holy Spirit to teach and lead me. It would also sabotage my authority as the spiritual leader of my family and in service to others. Slowly drifting away from my relationship with Jesus can be a very subtle thing—much like a marriage relationship that is slowly drifting apart without notice. The Holy Spirit is our guide, our helpmate, our teacher, our comforter, the lover of our souls, our provider and so much more.

One of my favorite ways to encourage people is to tell them God thinks about them all the time. Scripture proves God designed and created us, why we were created, that He had a plan for us from before the beginning of time, that He knew us before we were born and that we are in Jesus and He is in us. Three favorite Scripture passages which define my value are Psalm 139:16-18, Matthew 10:29-31 and Psalm 16:7-8.

One way that I encourage people through social media is by wishing them a happy birthday. The message I send looks something like this:

Wishing you a very happy birthday. Encouragement for your birthday comes from Psalm 32:7-8: "For you are my hiding place; you protect me from trouble. You surround me with songs of victory. The Lord says, 'I will guide you along the best pathway for your life. I will advise you and watch over you.'"

I'm blessed to discover that people get excited about those messages. They often respond with a thank you message or a social media like or love emoji. Some have even said they really needed the encouragement of that message. I often find that hearts are already prepared for the message of the Holy Spirit. Some have asked me how I come up with the Scriptures I send. That opens the door to talk about the ministry of the Holy Spirit, whom I consult before sending Scriptures. He generally gives me different Scriptures appropriate for the moment. It's never just the verse of the day that pops up in my Bible app. I reflect on the person, pray before selecting Scripture encouragement and often send verses from Psalms. These Scriptures are also from beautiful passages about how God loves us, forgives us and gives hope for the life yet to come. The Bible is just as relevant as it ever was. The Scriptures have definitely changed the way I think.

The point I'm making here is this: it was up to me to change. When the pain of life became greater than ignoring it, I surrendered who I thought I was in exchange for who Jesus said I am in His Word. I've often heard, "God can't move a parked car." Believing God about who I am was a decision I had to make. Once again, author Ted Dekker[1] sets the record straight in his book, The Forgotten Way:

But now I understood the heart of my search in a new way. It's all about identity, you see. Who are you? Really. You live for that discovery. And when you do, you will see that you are far more than you have imagined. Although I grew up in church and spent years studying theology, what I discovered in Jesus' teachings continued to stagger me. Once again, I wondered. How could I have missed the fundamental essence of His radically good news? How can I now possibly forget, and yet I do. As I've said, life consists of cycles of remembering and forgetting, and I, like you, still forget far too often, every time I get anxious or feel like a victim. And in that forgetting, my view is clouded once more until I remember who I am and surrender who I am not.

—Author Ted Dekker[8], The Forgotten Way

It's very difficult to carry out our purpose without obedience to the prompting of the Holy Spirit. Divine appointments are faith building experiences—proof positive of the power of God to help or encourage us and others.

IMMUTABLE PRINCIPLE #4 Every day, I will make an effort to shut down comparison with others. Comparing ourselves to the Scriptures is the best way to live a life of peace. Growing in my relationship with the Father, Son and Holy Spirit helps to define my faith purpose. I will get involved in ministry to others through a good Bible-believing church and community. Being involved is an important way to cultivate friendships and help others. I will be strengthened and encouraged in the process of helping others.

"Obviously, I'm not trying to win the approval of people, but of God. If pleasing people were my goal, I would not be Christ's servant." (Galatians 1:10)

PRAYER: Father in Heaven, I'm so grateful for the Scriptures that show me how comparison to others has created my defeating, defining inner language. Please forgive me, and set me on a path to change my way of thinking. Help me break out of the comparison net by discovering my purpose to encourage others in whatever ways You have planned for me. Remind me often so that I can keep Your Word in my heart. I pray this in Jesus' name, amen.

More hope lies ahead.

CHAPTER 4

BUCKET 1, BUCKET 2, AND BUCKET 3

Skills, Talents and Abilities

My older brother has many different skills, talents and abilities. In this chapter, I'll refer to them as gifts. He even plays the musical saw with a violin bow that is pulled upward against the edge of the saw to make a remarkable sound. We used to get together to play piano and musical saw duets. If I'm honest, I have to admit there was a time when I coveted his gifts. It would have been so helpful to have his aptitude to solve problems related to making home improvements. The sad truth is that I spent considerable time bemoaning the fact that I didn't have his skills. He could build houses, fix roofs, do kitchen and bathroom remodels and many other things. Another forte was writing up bids to seek jobs with commercial enterprises. He drew beautiful, artistic blueprints that he used in his work. His finish carpentry was extraordinary, and his attention to detail was impeccable. His work reputation was amazing, so much so that he didn't even need to advertise. Yet, his phone often rang with client referrals. Let's put my older brother's gifts in Bucket 1.

Whenever I compared my gifts to his, I came out on the short end of the stick, or at least that's what I believed. Whenever something would need repair at our home, I'd have to hire someone with Bucket 1 skills to come do the repairs. A couple of times, my brother generously brought his Bucket 1 gifts to our house to make repairs.

The sad truth is that I had no aptitude to fix or build things. I knew I could do a few things, but never considered them official gifts of much value. When I was in the seventh grade, the school required students to make some kind of project to be entered in the county fair. I decided my project would be a replica of the Seattle Space Needle. Another requirement was parent involvement. My dad, as you know, was a hard-working farmer. He probably didn't have time to help me, but he did. In fact, I didn't learn much from that project because dad built most of it, though I remember putting a few screws into the six thin laths used for the legs of the space needle. There's an old saying about situations like this: "If you have to carry the dog to catch the rabbit, you might as well catch the rabbit yourself." Dad did a great job, and the project won a blue ribbon. Maybe I wouldn't need a very big bucket, but let's put my gifts in Bucket 2.

One day, decades ago, after once again saying to my older brother, "I wish I had your skills," he replied, "You can do things I can't do." It never occurred to me that I could do valuable things others couldn't. How could that be true? From my point of view, my gifts seemed less valuable. The truth of my book's message must be shining through by now—affirming and nurturing childhood inner language needs to occur when children are young if possible. Whatever self-talk children learn will often be carried throughout life unless people determine to think differently about themselves according to what the Scriptures teach—though it's never too late to change how people think, no matter their age.

I thought that my Bucket 2 contents could not really be gifts from God. When the Scriptures that were "sharper than any two-edged sword" began to work in my spirit, I transitioned to my new way of thinking and living. I still don't have Bucket 1 skills, but that no longer matters. I can be blessed by others who do, and maybe even learn from them. It's about the attitude I have from day to day.

That brings us to you, the reader. Since I likely don't know you or what gifts you may have, I'm asking you to mentally place your gifts in Bucket 3. Look inside your bucket. What do you see? Do you consider yourself capable of doing a few things to get by, or do you feel you have valuable gifts you've used over time to help others? Have you received affirmation for what you've given to others? How does that feel? Consider the various ways you've used your gifts.

- How have you purposed your gifts to benefit yourself and hopefully others?
- Has comparison to others gotten in the way of your confidence to freely give of yourself?
- Are you developing your gifts to an even greater extent because you realize your God-given gifts have equipped you to fulfill your purpose?

Let's enjoy a bit of pure fantasy here. Imagine you see Buckets 1, 2 and 3 sitting six feet apart in the front of a room along a bare wall that contains each bucket's gifts. Picture these buckets being transformed into the people they represent—Bucket 1 as my older, skilled brother; Bucket 2, as me, the piano doodler and average student; and Bucket 3 as you, the reader who is either confident or not so confident about your gifts.

2 Corinthians 4:7 describes us as "fragile clay jars containing this great treasure" of belonging to Christ if we believe and have asked forgiveness for our sins. "This makes it clear that our great power is from God, not from ourselves." We've been given gifts to accomplish what "he planned for us long ago" (Ephesians 2:10). We live life from day to day in body, soul and spirit along with the gifts we carry within us.

Stop reading and ask yourself about your gifts. List them on a piece of paper in any order just as they come to you. Next, number your gifts in order of skill and interest level from highest to lowest. Here is a sample list to help you get started:

Good at business	Excellent organizer
Great planner	Skilled construction worker
Awesome parent	Gifted musician
Good writer	Gifted teacher
Skilled gardener	Pastor

Next, decide which are among your top three gifts. Let's call your top three gifts your purpose. The goal is for you to serve others, using your purpose. How have you used your top three gifts in service to others? Remember, you have been given a gift(s) (1 Peter 4:10-11) to serve others.

I've already said that when I acknowledged my gifts are from God, it opened up an entirely new attitude about serving others, and it was no bother at all. Acknowledging my gifts meant praying and thanking God for what I had been given. It also meant I had to tell God I was willing to be led by the Holy Spirit in the use of my gifts, and that I would do my best to develop what He's given me. The depth and effectiveness of my service to others increased as I decreased my belief that I had nothing to offer to others. I have a new sense of empowerment when I share my gifts with others (Acts 1:8).

James 2:26 says, "As the body without the spirit is dead, so faith without deeds is dead." There he goes again. James is always right on point. But what did he mean when he wrote that? Think of it this way: Deeds are closely related to purpose. It's not that we have to earn our salvation. If that were the case, grace and forgiveness would have no place in why Christ died—for the forgiveness of our sins. "But if we confess our sins to him, he is faithful and just to forgive us our sins and to cleanse us from all wickedness" (1 John 1:9).

"Now someone may argue, 'Some people have faith; others have good deeds.' But I say, 'How can you show me your faith if you don't have good deeds? I will show you my faith by my good deeds'" (James 2:18). Ouch! So good deeds are the result of our purpose, not that we could earn the free gift of forgiveness of our sins and the salvation of our souls. Our love for Jesus drives us to make a difference in the world by helping and ministering to others; that age-old adage to "Leave the world better off than when you arrived" fits here. Besides that, a gigantic promise is associated with our purpose found in 1 Corinthians 15:58: "So, my dear brothers and sisters, be strong and immovable. Always work enthusiastically for the Lord, for you know that nothing you do for the Lord is ever useless."

Those lesser gifts you have are still of value too. As you practice them, you'll be able to recognize situations where you can share even your lesser gifts. This is another reason for walking in the Spirit (Galatians 5:25), to hone the skill of listening for the impressions of the Holy Spirit in our inner thoughts. Jesus said, "My sheep know my voice" (John 10:27-28).

Consider the spiritual gift of helps. Those with this gift are people who serve joyfully behind the scenes without much recognition. It could be helping a neighbor without expecting payment. Helps people might babysit, do work at church, or run an errand for someone, for example. There's no end to this kind of service. These people would much rather be unnoticed. (Colossians 3:23-24)

We've already established the truth that God doesn't favor one over the other. Rather than think in the old ways of inadequacy, accept who you are. Cultivate your gift(s), believe God's purpose for your life, and commit to helping others. There's way too much to know, for any of us to know everything. That's why we each have specific gifts. The gifts we already have are enough to accomplish God's purpose for our lives. Could someone look inside your Bucket 3 and think, "Wow, those are Bucket 1 gifts—such valuable skills." We see our gifts only through the lens of our thoughts, but someone needs help with the gifts in our bucket. We must understand that comparison to others can kill us inside, leaving us to think we have very little of value to offer, even to God who created us in the first place. We are not His mistake.

The more we use our gifts, the more we'll be able to develop other gifts in our bucket to contribute toward others. What we contribute to others may also become our livelihood. We have to love ourselves because we're supposed to love our neighbor as we love who we are. Scripture proves it. When God approached Moses to be a leader, he said he couldn't do it because he stammered and wasn't a good speaker. Yet God enabled Moses to fulfill His purpose. When we feel like we're not enough for a task, God is with us to help us, and He will do that if we ask Him to.

When I was a boy, I knew I had an interest in music. It wasn't that I recognized myself as a virtuoso. In fact, I often told myself I couldn't do it. My older sister played piano much better than I. She was very diligent at practicing and had been taking lessons longer. I, on the other hand, was a doodler—someone who spent time figuring out what sounded great rather than practicing very much. Over time, I developed my ability to hear sounds and chord structures. Someone once asked me why I couldn't be more like my sister. I felt frustrated and defeated, unable to excel in music. The truth is that it would have been easy to give up hope of playing the piano. I certainly didn't know about giftedness as a child nor for many years of my adulthood.

Little by little, I began to think I might be able to achieve my boyhood desire of becoming a musician. My identity was wrapped up in playing piano so I could hopefully receive the affirmation I needed. Unfortunately, that identity was misplaced thinking. Through the spiritual renaissance provided by the Holy Scriptures and ministry of the Holy Spirit, my full identity is now in Jesus Christ who gave me the gifts to fulfill God's purposes. Eventually, I enrolled in piano lessons in college and continued to slowly improve my skills, though

I'm still a doodler at heart. The gift of music and doodling actually paid off in 2019 when I released a piano album of old hymns and worship songs, *Grace & the Cross*. I played all of the songs on the album without written music except for one song, and even that song was my own arrangement. Though I can't play jazz-style piano, I play with a lot of the chords you might hear in jazz music. So, you see, if you've been given a gift from God, please develop it. Work at it. Practice it. Whatever you practice and have an interest in can be used to fulfill a purpose that results in good deeds that glorify God. Though affirmation and accolades for our deeds are rewarding, it's more important to "let your good deeds shine out for all to see, so that everyone will praise your heavenly Father" (Matthew 5:16). Doing that is proof that we acknowledge God as the source and purpose of our gifts.

A friend I'll call Suzanne tells the harrowing story about her struggle to release her God-given gifts under some very dark circumstances:

I'm not sure when it began, I just know that at an early age I became aware of the darkness. It began as a sadness that eventually grew into crushing despair filled with rage and torment. I was alone. No one understood. Early on, I tried to find help by talking to teachers and counselors, but eventually this wasn't enough as talking and crying didn't make the hurt in my heart stop or the darkness go away. I turned to self-mutilation—somehow the physical pain took the edge off, and the wounds and blood made people listen. I spent five years in and out of mental hospitals, and each time I was diagnosed with a different mental illness and treated with different medications—none of which provided answers or made the pain go away. Toward the end, I came to the conclusion that no matter how far I ran, I would never be able to escape the torment I felt because it was inside of me. Over time, the self-mutilation ultimately morphed into suicide attempts.

In the midst of all of this, I graduated from high school in the top 10% of my class. I was voted the most talented by my peers and went on to study piano in college. Yet none of my achievements seemed to matter. The message I heard from others was that I had much unrealized potential. But they couldn't understand that it didn't matter how much potential I had when on the inside I was so desperate for peace. I was involved in church, youth group and Bible study, but could never find comfort in what I learned. Instead, it only seemed to make what was going on inside of me worse—condemnation at every turn, never measuring up and with no hope for escape.

All along the way, God put people in my life who helped me to stay alive until I could fully hear and accept His message. I met a friend who, in one of my darkest moments, prayed with me and explained not how my actions were so terrible, or catered to my own self-loathing, but showed me what God thought of me and the deep love He had for me. We prayed that He would bring me the help I needed. The next day, I learned about Teen Challenge and audibly heard the voice of God telling me to go. And that began my journey to freedom. It didn't come all at once. I first had to learn the difference between grace and the Old Testament Law. Then I was introduced to the Holy Spirit and received His baptism. This is when my eyes were truly opened to the darkness surrounding me, and I was given the power in Jesus' name to make it flee. Then, I had to learn about who Jesus really was and how to have a relationship with Him. Suddenly, I wasn't alone. He was with me. He understood everything and didn't look at me with shame or judgment. The despair lifted, and my heart began to heal—I finally had peace.

This journey started almost twenty years ago, and I am still walking with Jesus and living in His peace. The Lord's plans for my life are far greater than anything I could hope for, His power is stronger than anything the enemy might throw at me and His love is so much deeper than any pain I might experience. He is my hope to overcome all that seeks to destroy me. The promise of Isaiah 43:2 is my comfort. "When you go through deep waters, I will be with you. When you go through rivers of difficulty, you will not drown. When you walk through the fire of oppression, you will not be burned up; the flames will not consume you."

Thanks for sharing your personal story, Suzanne.

There are probably very few people who have not experienced a dark period at some point in their lives. People who have experienced emotional darkness may sometimes realize their pain is actually connected to fear. Fear can be a good thing in the context of protecting or warning us about life's most dangerous situations. Yet, fear can also profoundly cripple us and prevent us from accomplishing things within our grasp—maybe a new career, relationship, or ministry, for example. I spent much of my early life and some of my adult life paralyzed by fear because I lacked the confidence to believe in my own capabilities. It could be about fear of being rejected by peers, fear of failure, fear of retribution, fear of an accident or a medical condition. The sources of fear are endless. The trouble with fear is that those around us often have no idea what we're going through, and most people won't ask for help from others. When we refuse to ask for help, we deny others the chance to use their gifts. What will they think of me if I appear to be weak and lack confidence? Fear. (2 Corinthians 1:3-7)

You know I came from a farming background. Let me tell you about a man who leased farmland from the land owner. The terms of a farm lease can vary, but this particular lease included an old farmhouse. The lease required sharing the proceeds from the crops and sometimes sharing farming expenses with the landowner. The landowner had no responsibility to work the farm he'd leased to the farmer. I share this story to illustrate how the fear of investment can overpower someone's desire to own their own property.

The farmer noticed his neighbor's adjoining farm was for sale. It seemed like such a natural and logical decision to purchase the neighboring farm, but fear overtook him. He believed it wouldn't be possible to purchase the land because he wouldn't be able to pay out, meaning he believed the farm was too expensive to buy without the risk of defaulting on the mortgage. Unfortunately, the farmer failed to see the possible potential if he were to apply his excellent skills to his neighbor's farm. Nor did he have the vision to see the farm as an investment for his golden years.

Here is the saddest part of the farmer's story. His farming gifts were unsurpassed. The crops he planted and harvested were beautiful. He could fix or build anything he needed to accomplish his work. With a full bucket of farming gifts to make purchasing the neighbor's farm a reality, he still couldn't do it. He was just too afraid. And that's the reason the farmer's retirement investments were not enough to sustain him in his old age.

From the Parable of the Talents in Matthew 25, we learn about investing our time and talents in wise ways. The return on our investment is largely connected to the amount we're willing to invest. If we keep a lid on our bucket and don't use our God-given gifts, no one will benefit from them. Think about it this way. What would happen if you were to tip over your bucket and spill out your gifts? Would you personally benefit from releasing your gifts? Who else would be blessed if you were to release your gifts in service to others? Ephesians 3:12 tells us, "In him and through faith in him we may approach God with freedom and confidence." Our gifts are to be used to help ourselves and others, and to glorify our Heavenly Father. Let go!

IMMUTABLE PRINCIPLE #5: I will identify the gifts, interests and aptitudes I've been given, develop and use my gifts to help others and never give up.

IMMUTABLE PRINCIPLE #6: I will accept my gifts as from God and be grateful for them.

"But Moses pleaded with the Lord, 'O Lord, I'm not very good with words. I never have been, and I'm not now, even though you have spoken to me. I get tongue-tied, and my words get tangled.' Then the Lord asked Moses, 'Who makes a person's mouth? Who decides whether people speak or do not speak, hear or do not hear, see or do not see? Is it not I, the Lord?'" (Exodus 4:10-11)

PRAYER: Dear Heavenly Father, I ask that You would help me identify and accept the gifts You've given me with thanksgiving, that I may glorify You and help those You put in my path. I also ask that You help me identify any selfish way in me that would not honor You. I pray these things in the holy name of Jesus, amen.

Hope is life-changing. Watch for it. Be available to accept it. Let the truth of Scripture and the Holy Spirit change you.

CHAPTER 5

THE LETTER S

Shame and Shaming
Discovering Purpose

This chapter is brought to you by the letter S. Digging into the meaning and causes for today's S-word may be somewhat painful to examine. This S stands for...get ready for it...shame. I didn't want to write about shame, but it's the next big realization in the sequence of the inner language we've talked about thus far. When I was growing up, it was mostly the adults who seemed to control me by causing shame when I was guilty of kid crimes. Come to think of it, adults probably shamed other adults as well, but that wasn't my world. I grew up in a generation that found it acceptable to say *Shame on you,* or *You should be ashamed of yourself,* or *It's a shame you did whatever.* Do people still say those kinds of things to their children? I certainly hope not.

In my childhood, people used shame as a method of control. Theoretically, if I felt bad enough, I'd stop doing whatever it was that was bugging the adult in the room. Shaming didn't begin with my parents' generation, but likely from many generations earlier.

It wasn't just parents who would use those shaming words either. Teachers in the public school also said those words. Again, it was all about control in the accepted cultural standard of the day. Shame worked to address all kinds of situations and delivered in different ways—the glaring look, the shaming words, the corporal punishment, the grounding. My crimes ranged from not cleaning up my dinner plate all the way up the continuum of shame to flagrant disobedience. The result was the same—the degree of stupidity or worthlessness was linked to the severity of the offense and the words used to bring about the shame.

I remember even as an adult being shamed for being too thin. Of course, I wasn't too thin according to my height and weight. The person doing the shaming was morbidly obese. Though I'm no psychologist, I believe that the many times I've been successful with weight loss and then gained all the weight back is directly connected to that person. I mentioned Mark Wolynn's book, *It Didn't Start With You*, in Chapter 1. Remember that a stronghold in a person's life is something that prevents them from doing the right thing.

Words spoken to children can either tear them down or build them up. It's the same for adults, of course. Even when comments spoken seem to be neutral, the person on the receiving end is left to wonder about the speaker's meaning and purpose for saying those words. I've known naturally suspicious people, perhaps because they've had to be, who truly assumed the worst.

Brené Brown[9], well-known shame researcher and entertaining TED Talk speaker, boiled it down this way: *Guilt = I did something bad. Shame = I am bad.* How could something as complex as shame be so simply explained?

Think of this progression of events:
1. Comparison to others
2. Judgment about whether a person measured up to the comparison
3. Negative inner language formed, dependent on judgment
4. Guilt determined by the inner language that results
5. Shame determined by the response to guilt

If someone were to say, *that was a really stupid thing to do*, guilt turns to shame almost immediately: *I am stupid. I have no value.* People's inner language may also say *that was a really stupid thing to do*. Someone who receives and practices shame as part of their everyday life builds up a bank of words, leaving them paralyzed, unable to conclude that they are anything but worthless. They actually believe something is wrong with them. People like that have lived in shame so long that they can't break free to think differently. It's the lie they've told themselves because of the accumulating inner language brought on first by comparing themselves to others, then by repeated shaming. Self-shaming can be so harmful that paranoia can eventually develop if they don't seek help. When people constantly live in shame, it can make them question their relevance, and that may lead to depression. Gratefully, my adult life has been very rewarding, though a true feeling of success came much later. I didn't yet understand why I couldn't feel more successful.

I'm sure I adopted and used shaming in raising our own children to a certain extent—something I shouldn't have done, but I hadn't yet processed that information. After all, others modeled it as the standard of discipline for me. Unless we're aware of the practice, we're doomed to repeat it from generation to generation. So, how can we approach this differently than *That was really a stupid thing to do?*

This simple dialogue illustrates how to lessen or avoid shaming.

"I noticed all the apples in the basement had spilled out of the box. How did that happen?" Listen for their response. Then, "Together, let's find a solution. How could this problem be fixed?" Listen for their response, and lead them to conclude it would be good to pick up the apples. "That's an acceptable solution except for one thing—a few of the apples are bruised. What can be done to solve that part of the problem?" Listen for their response, leading them to the idea that they need to pay for the damage if necessary. "Yes, I agree. It would be fair to pay for the bruised apples. Either one dollar from your allowance or piggy bank works for me. Which would you choose?" Wait for their response. "Thanks for helping us solve this problem. I love you. You've made some good choices today."

Making a child pay for damages is probably a little excessive, depending on the age and demeanor of the child. I used it in this example to illustrate how the right words can make a huge difference. Notice how I never once used the word *you*. Instead, I used the words *we* and *us*, which meant we were on the same team, working together to find a solution without blame. *You* can sound very accusing and produce guilt, only adding to the negative reinforcement.

I also didn't use the word *stupid* in that line of questioning, yet I held the child to a standard of behavior and expectation, with no hint of humiliation or condemnation. Rather, I chose to use words that showed respect and honor. Imagine that my voice tone was loving rather than condemning.

Years ago, I had a superintendent of schools who had a terrific way of dealing with people. Parents would sometimes be very angry when they arrived for a meeting with him. But they would almost always leave smiling or even laughing, while thanking him and shaking hands. It made no sense how this could possibly be, so I asked him about it. He explained, "Well, you can say whatever needs to be said as long as you choose the right words."

That's how it is with both children and adults. If parents use words to empower their children to make good decisions, children won't feel the condemnation that quickly transforms into shame. Heaping shame on a child may control their behavior, but over time, it will impact their self-worth. It might also help to offer choices.

Imagine going to a child two weeks later and saying, "Today I was thinking again about those spilled apples in the basement. I couldn't help but remember how proud I was that you were able to solve that problem. Just thought I'd let you know. You're such a good kid!"

Children who aren't allowed to make simple decisions as children find it hard to make increasingly complex decisions as they mature into adulthood. Letting children fail with grace teaches them how to succeed. Wise parents will give opportunities to practice making decisions. When children fail, brainstorm about why they failed, using examples of good choices. Say things like, "Next time you could either pick up the apples or ask someone for help. Or perhaps you can think of an even better option." Such statements show honor and respect for a child.

I still remember shaming events that happened to me as a child. As mentioned, we remember events that reach our emotions. At about age ten, as inquisitive boys will do, I found an aluminum 90-degree elbow pipe on the farm, the kind possibly used for venting air outside, and I was very curious about what might fit in that elbow. I remembered my mom had rows of canning jars for preserving fruit in our dank-smelling, dimly lit  cellar. Though I knew they were off limits, I went down the four stairs leading to the cellar and pushed open the squeaky door, grabbed a pint jar off the shelf, and quickly ran outside to try to fit it in that elbow pipe. It fit perfectly— too perfectly actually. The pint jar became stuck in one end of the elbow, and no amount of pulling or prying would loosen it. I felt sick inside with fear of really getting in trouble. Fear is a miserable feeling because, in this case, I projected shame for creating the problem in the first place. I now confess that I hid the pint jar and the elbow in the bushes behind our old farmhouse, so that no one ever knew or talked about it—ever. How could I have been so stupid? It gets to be a vicious circle for some people. Shame becomes self-imposed because self-worth is missing.

One warm spring day, Dad took me to a field in his brown Ford F-150 pickup down the road from the shop. My job was to pull a heavy iron roller (a piece of farm equipment) behind our red Ferguson 135 diesel tractor to pack down the soil in a recently planted field. The new crop had already emerged in straight green rows a week earlier. I got on the tractor seat, and Dad got on the side step to ride along, leaning against the fender next to me. He wanted to show me the work to be done for the first couple rounds before leaving to do his own work back at the shop. I was probably about fourteen years old at the time.

After several rounds pulling the heavy, noisy roller, I decided to put the tractor in a higher gear so I could finish the work faster…and finish faster I did…too fast, in fact! My dad noticed I'd walked back to the shop where he was working. "You aren't finished already, are you?" he asked. Yes, I was finished all right. He was not happy at all, saying I may have damaged the newly emerging plants. I don't remember what he said after that, but I remember how I had disappointed him. How could I have been so stupid?

When I was in college working on my BA, one of my professors decided to put the recently scored exams in rank order from highest to lowest. The next time we met, he said, "I was able to score your exams." He proceeded to put the stack of papers on the table. "These exams are in order from highest to lowest score. As I call your name, come up and get your exam." If I remember right, the professor also announced the score for each student as our names were called. Can you imagine the humiliation of the last few students as they picked up their papers? How could such a thing have been allowed at a university? Do you suppose those last students began to feel shame as the stack of exams dwindled? I did. My paper was near the bottom of the stack. I felt terribly humiliated in front of my peers.

My early college days were quite challenging. I had to balance a twenty-hour work week with a full credit load every quarter, and I just didn't have the confidence I needed to be successful. While writing this book, I wondered how my early college days might have been different had I been equipped with the right inner language.

Then, something very special happened to cause me to think differently. It was the fourth Sunday in September, and I'd been scheduled to play the organ for church. The service had barely begun when a tall, beautiful girl with long blonde hair walked into the sanctuary with her parents in the university town where I was raised. I noticed where she and her parents sat on the left near the back. After the last Amen of the service, I walked briskly into the hallway to find her—she was even prettier up close. I introduced myself and enjoyed visiting with her parents as well. There were some déjà vu moments when I realized her last name was one my parents had fondly referred to as I was growing up. Indeed, I realized she was related to four people my parents had known for decades. Her family had a wheat farm in north central Washington, ten miles from her hometown. Our farm was ten miles from my hometown too. Her parents had brought her to the university to begin her freshman year. I thought. This meeting might have potential.

Ten days later, we went on our first date—a motorcycle ride up in the mountains. Within a few days, I learned she had been valedictorian of her graduating class. My heart sank for the moment, thinking how intelligent she must be compared to me. More shaming. Did I mention that she was beautiful? From that point on, I was quite

 successful in college. Shame is a powerful emotion and motivator. The old negative inner language was still hidden, but my reputation was at stake here. I tried harder to be a better student. Fast forward two years later to June 7, the date I graduated from the university, and just a week later to June 14, the date of our wedding.

Now, I was a husband who needed a teaching job. After four separate interviews in different school districts, one of them offered me a contract near my wife's hometown. After successfully teaching for three years, I entered graduate school to earn a Master's Degree. Three years after completing my Masters, I entered graduate school again, this time to obtain administrative credentials, earning good grades in both programs. One day on the way to class, my professor walked up beside me. "You're really changing," he said. What did he mean by that statement? "Your writing is showing great professional growth since the beginning of the quarter." I had two or three papers to write every week. By that time, I was sure I had no words left to write. That comment was filed away for life. It had reached my emotions.

It had been a long, somewhat crooked path, but the feeling of those accomplishments was something I will never forget. A year later, I was offered and accepted an elementary principal position. Regardless of all those successes, underneath I still struggled with a lack of confidence that had never been formally identified or addressed. My wife would tell me I seemed confident when she would see me working at school. She sometimes came for special events or board presentations. With an outgoing personality, my career seemed to be thriving. As explained in Chapter 3, I was caught in the net of comparison to others. I should have said to myself, *You have accomplished so much.* But for now, my focus was on the energy and direction required for everyday life and career.

By that time, we had two amazing children, and I loved being their dad. They are still our best friends today. We were active in our church, especially in choral music ministry and teaching.

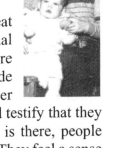

For twenty-seven years, we developed great relationships with friends and relatives. Our annual Easter and Christmas choral musical presentations were beautiful gifts of ministry to the community made possible by extraordinary vocal talents and the power of the Holy Spirit. After every concert, people would testify that they had been drawn closer to God. When God's Spirit is there, people sense it and feel inspired, knowing God is in control. They feel a sense of peace and wellbeing. At the time I felt God's guiding presence in my life, but had no idea what was yet to come. (Galatians 5:25)

After seven years as an elementary principal, I shifted to the district's central office to learn Special Programs Administration. It was a challenging move, to say the least. I wrote successful government grants, secured funding for district-wide network access and managed all district, state and federal special programs. During an administrative meeting one day, the high school principal said he recognized that I'd worked hard, and that I should, in essence, be proud of all that I had accomplished. Again, this was a comment that reached my emotions. Why couldn't I honestly acknowledge all that was good in my life and family as blessings from God? Those were years of very hard work. I still felt an unnamed source of weakness, the knowledge that I was still not good enough.

It's reasonable to assume no one is exempt from shame of varying kinds. But what about self-inflicted shame? Here's a hypothetical example that is not so hypothetical:

That chocolate cake with cream cheese frosting and sprinkles looks so good. Okay, I'll have a piece—then guilt followed by shame followed by another piece of cake followed by more guilt and shame. I've already been bad once, so I might as well have another piece. Half a cake later, the self-condemnation is shame. I'm sorry to have eaten that much cake. Now I don't feel very well.

Our rational minds are capable of doing irrational things. It's surprising what people will do when enough variables come together at one time. We can think of all the reasons why we shouldn't act on an irrational thought, but the desire to do so can be so immensely powerful that acting on the irrational thought sometimes wins out. This internal war with self has been going on for a very long time. The Apostle Paul addressed the problem in Romans 7:15 when he said, "I don't really understand myself, for I want to do what is right, but I don't do it. Instead, I do what I hate." Paul answered his own conundrum in Romans 7:24-25: "Oh, what a miserable person I am! Who will free me from this life that is dominated by sin and death? Thank God! The answer is in Jesus Christ our Lord. So, you see how it is: In my mind I really want to obey God's law, but because of my sinful nature I am a slave to sin."

Without question, some of the shame I experienced was the result of the decisions I made—I'd brought it on myself. I've ranted about how awful it feels to have someone inflict shame upon me. But the truth is that self-inflicted shame feels just as bad, maybe even worse, than any other kind of shame.

Shame creates a sense of vulnerability. The process of writing this book has created the feeling that I've really exposed myself to the world, revealing my innermost thoughts and feelings, my life struggles, my woundedness, my career, my successes and failures, my faith and purpose. What kind of guy does that? What a weak, emotional person I've shown you through my writing, even though those weaknesses and vulnerabilities were probably not visible to those on the outside. After all, I didn't pay much attention to my insecurity while raising our family or during my career. A person just does what's required each day.

Maybe you've heard the term *"thorn in the flesh."* Not having inner confidence was definitely mine—and I'm sure there are hundreds like me. Everyone has a thorn in the flesh, though who talks about that? It feels far too vulnerable to expose our inner weaknesses to others, yet Paul spoke of having a thorn in the flesh. He expressed the pain of his weakness in 2 Corinthians 12:7b-9: "So, to keep me from becoming proud, I was given a thorn in my flesh, a messenger from Satan to torment me and keep me from becoming proud. Three different times I begged the Lord to take it away. Each time he said, 'My grace is all you need. My power works best in weakness.' So now I am glad to boast about my weaknesses, so that the power of Christ can work through me."

What? I can be vulnerable and strong at the same time? There is an undeniable truth here if we're able to grasp it. When I stopped relying on myself and started relying on God, my strength began to return. It's an uncanny concept whereby we give up our private inner self in exchange for a relationship with, and dependence on, God. It's a peace the world can't give. Since God is omniscient, my private self was not a secret to Him anyway.

After having written with such transparency, consider the contrast between strength and weakness. This concept is contrary to both how we think and what our culture has taught us. In the very next verse, 2 Corinthians 12:10, Paul continued. "That is why, for Christ's sake, I delight in weaknesses, in insults, in hardships, in persecutions, in difficulties. For when I am weak, then I am strong." In baring my soul to the reader for the express purpose of helping others to see themselves as God sees them, I am made stronger because I have confessed that God has the ability to change me. If I hadn't been obedient to the Holy Spirit to write, I might still be stuck in my old way of thinking—which is that I'm not enough.

Here's how a friend I'll call Barbara described her thorn in the flesh:

"This past year has been a time of reflection for me—reflection upon my past and the way it had such an impact on the woman I've become. Through this process, I realized I have held a lot of personal judgment against myself, stemming from different points in my life when I felt ashamed—shame about who I was, what I looked like and how I came to be.

Some of this came from what people said about me...how I looked, what I wore, where I grew up, even how I began life. At a very young age, I was told I was a mistake. Looking back on this, I know the intention of the person who told me was not to hurt me. Rather, the point was to describe someone who had been conceived out of wedlock. It wasn't that I personally was the mistake, but that my birth was unintended. That was the beginning of my journey to prove that I was not a mistake. That shame was the driving force behind my efforts to be successful and my way to prove others wrong about who I am. I often tried to defend my parents' ability to raise a woman to be someone. This turned out to be a larger undertaking than I thought. Life does not always go as one plans.

Throughout my teenage and young adult years, I continued to run into people who judged me in the same ways I judged myself. By the time I reached my twenties, my self-esteem was extremely low. I realized through a bad relationship in college that I had defined myself by what others thought of me or let others define who they wanted me to be. Although my life appears successful from the outside—I have a career, a family, and a husband—I still struggle with feelings of inadequacy. Every single day, I have to turn this over to God. I take heart in knowing we are all imperfect beings, and we all struggle with something in our lives; but God still deeply loves us. It's my calling to help others who struggle with shame and fear of judgment as I do. My purpose is to help them realize they can drop their façade and be just who God made them to be."

Thanks for sharing your personal story, Barbara.

Everyone has a down day once in a while, but sometimes people experience months of discouragement. When this happens, we need help. What is the antidote? Here's a possible common scenario to explore:

At work you've noticed there seems to be tension building between you and another coworker. The tension is largely kept under the surface, but it's definitely there. As time passes, you realize your inner turmoil is starting to affect your health. A friend reaches out to you. "Seems like something is bothering you." You pour out the whole story of anxiety about the work tension. The friend responds, "I certainly understand how you feel. When I worked in your area last year, I felt that same tension. After a while, I realized the tension I felt was a result of my coworker's own anxiety. I learned he and his spouse were contemplating making a serious personal decision. When I understood their circumstances, I became much more empathetic toward them. My focus changed from myself and how I felt, to my anxious coworker. When I responded with kindness and understanding, I received kindness in return. Empathy is a powerful tool in dissolving shame. (See 2 Corinthians 1:3-7.) I hope that helped you. Let me know if you ever need to talk about this again. You're a valuable employee."

We can receive empathy from others, and we can even give ourselves empathy. Our self-talk will change as the Scriptures provide us empathy and understanding. I try to spend quiet times meditating on the Scriptures every day. My favorite kind of empathy and encouragement comes from the Scriptures. The Holy Spirit uses the Scriptures to help strengthen my resolve to have a positive, Scriptural outlook. God's Word contains many empathetic Scripture verses. Try this online search: empathetic Scriptures. Such Scriptures have the power to encourage and to heal us. The Holy Spirit also uses the Scriptures to teach or speak to us by sending thoughtful impressions to our minds. Let the power of the Holy Spirit speak to your soul as you quietly sense His presence. Whenever possible, I literally visualize these verses from Psalm 40 so as to place myself in the setting: "He set my feet on solid ground and steadied me as I walked along."

Though I hate to admit it, I believe there are evil people who do evil things. Are evil people evil because they carry so much personal shame? Is it because they have had an insufferable life marked by staggering emotional pain? Would evil people have become evil had they not been molested repeatedly over a period of several years? If an evil person had been nurtured and raised in a loving home with compassion and understanding, would they still have become evil? It's impossible to know these answers. Remember Brené Brown's definition? *Guilt = I did something bad. Shame = I am bad.* If shame is allowed to multiply, hope diminishes significantly. Without a faith conversion to believe in Jesus, or at the very least, professional counseling, hope is quite elusive. Last Easter season, our theme at church was taken from a newer worship song, *Hope Has a Name*[10]. Jesus is our blessed hope.

Seldom do I have the sensation of shame unless Satan attacks me with condemnation. The Lord of heaven's armies is there to intercede for us. "Who then will condemn us? No one—for Christ Jesus died for us and was raised to life for us, and he is sitting in the place of honor at God's right hand, interceding for us" (Romans 8:34).

Guilt may be a factor if I've done something wrong. Yes, it's still possible I could do something wrong—I sometimes do. But grace and forgiveness for those times is made possible by Jesus' death on the cross. Jesus literally took my shame for me when He died for my sins. As Paul the Apostle wrote, "The answer is in Jesus Christ our Lord."

The author of the Book of Hebrews explained the Christian life in Hebrews 12:1-2: "Therefore, since we are surrounded by such a huge crowd of witnesses to the life of faith, let us strip off every weight that slows us down, especially the sin that so easily trips us up." I simply failed to realize who the Scriptures say I am. It says I've been forgiven. "And let us run with endurance the race God has set before us." The race I'm running is now marked with purpose. "We do this by keeping our eyes on Jesus," not being distracted by life's problems or what's going on in the world, but depending on our faith in Jesus…"the champion who initiates and perfects our faith. Because of the joy awaiting him, he endured the cross, disregarding its shame." I don't have to live in shame. I can live in peace. "Now he is seated in the place of honor beside God's throne." I imagine how God, the Father, "will order his angels to protect me wherever I go." (Psalm 91:11)

IMMUTABLE PRINCIPLE #7: If I feel shame, I will immediately cast it off as inconsistent with who the Scriptures say I am. If necessary, I will ask forgiveness of Jesus and anyone I may have wronged in order to minimize or stop the shame. It's clear that the antidote for shame is empathy, so I will memorize Scriptures like Ephesians 2:10, 1 Peter 4:10-11 and Romans 12:1-2 to remind me of my value to God.

"Give all your worries and cares to God, for he cares about you." (1 Peter 5:7)

PRAYER: Thank You, Heavenly Father, that I have learned the way of life that means living with purpose without condemnation. I'm asking You to strengthen my resolve each day to live in Your peace made possible by Your grace, forgiveness and love. In Jesus' name, Amen.

There's more and more hope ahead.

CHAPTER 6

MAY I HAVE THE ENVELOPE PLEASE?

New Inner Language

Remember how Jesus spoke in stories or parables? After all, it was Jesus' most commonly used teaching method. He would sometimes provide time for people who were listening to ask questions about the story too. Using this same method, imagine a story where you, as the reader, are recognized at an awards ceremony.

Your excitement has been building for weeks, knowing you are scheduled to go to a major faith-based recognition ceremony in Los Angeles. This recognition ceremony highlights the spiritual growth of individuals and church groups who are advancing the cause of Christ.

Finally, the day arrives when you drive to the airport to board the plane for a long flight to LAX. You check into the hotel so you can change into what you hope is appropriate clothing. A taxi arrives to take you to the famous Faith Center Theater.

You are greeted by a wide red carpet reserved only for famous people, yet you are allowed to walk to the theater entrance as if you are one of those people. It certainly makes you wonder. "Is my name on some qualifying list of *red-carpet people*?" And then it starts.

Photographers whisper, perhaps wondering if they should take your photograph. How are they to know? It all seems unbelievable as first one and then another photographer starts clicking their cameras. Maybe they're taking photographs of everyone. You're feeling thankful that you brought the right clothes.

Once inside, you realize the Faith Center Theater is regal in every way, much more so than what you remember from previous recognition ceremonies seen on television. Some very well-known people of faith are seated around dinner tables, some of whom you recognize as famous because of their national organizations. You feel a little sheepish at first before you remember that you're trying to overcome the temptation to compare.

The Master of Ceremonies is about to come to the microphone to begin the proceedings. It's going to be a great night. Will you be selected for recognition? Will there be lots of competition in your category? As the process goes on, the MC gives out awards to many others, which only raises your angst about how this is going to play out.

Every time the MC announces a name, that person responds with a short thank you speech, recognizing those who played a significant role in their success. Some people even share their personal testimonies.

"Up next," the Master of Ceremonies finally announces, "is the recognition for the Most Improved Inner Language." A surprised whisper goes through the audience. This is the first year the governing board has allowed this category.

You wonder how many others will be receiving recognition in your category. Have you improved enough to be recognized when there are so many others in the theater?

"This recognition is given to the candidate who has accepted a biblical way of thinking about who they are," the MC continues. "The recognition will be given to a candidate who has consistently changed their inner language according to the following criteria:

1. *They believe they are God's masterpiece. (Ephesians 2:10)*
2. *They understand that God thinks about them according to Psalm 139:1-18.*

3. *They believe God lifts them up when they are discouraged according to Psalm 40:1-5.*
4. *They believe shame can be overcome with empathy and forgiveness. (1 John 1:9)*
5. *They understand what it means to listen for impressions from the Holy Spirit. (John 10:27)*
6. *They develop new life purpose resulting in good deeds. (James 2:18)*

"May I have the envelope please? The candidates for the most advanced change to their inner language are…" He reads your name and stops…there are no other names because you have no competition. He continues, "And the winner is…" Your name is called, and the audience erupts with cheers and applause.

You find it strange that no other candidates are being considered in your category. Maybe they don't realize how wonderful it is to be truly free to live out God's purposes. You realize your genre is not a competition at all—that you really haven't won anything except the recognition. And then you're struck by a cathartic thought. You have a new way of thinking and a new way of life. You truly are a winner after all.

The truth of what has just happened is beginning to set in. Your new inner language is between you and God alone. It's time for you to step to the podium to give your acceptance speech. As you do, you are handed a recognition certificate. Your throat begins to tighten as you prepare to speak. Your confidence rises exponentially when you remember that you think differently now. You realize what's happening is God's purpose for you, even though you feel a bit exposed to be sharing such private thoughts about your inner language.

"I'd like to thank God for helping me to understand how my former way of thinking was not a healthy way to live," you say, speaking with confidence. "I've changed because of the Scriptures and the impressions I've felt from the Holy Spirit. The more I have practiced my new way of thinking, the easier it has become. I have discovered a new purpose in life—to have a deeper, more personal relationship with Jesus. Thank you."

You hope that perhaps the initial recognition in this category will at least bring awareness to this new way of life so that maybe next year others will desire to change the way they think about who they are.

You recall your old way of thinking and how it impacted your life since you were a child. It was a crippling way to live. Then, without warning, your thoughts turn to how others could be transformed if they only knew how. Every single candidate who has been transformed by the Scriptures and the Holy Spirit would be on that stage. (Matthew 6:33) The marvelous truth is that we never have to compete for God's affection. He loves each of us more than we could even imagine, and His deepest desire is to transform us. In fact, Scripture says that He offers the truth to anyone with ears to hear and hearts to receive. And it's not just about your transformation. It's given to us in order to bless others—making us change agents for the benefit of others.

After two more recognition categories, the orchestra begins to play as the audience moves toward the exits. It's been an exciting night. You have a sense of praise and thankfulness as you flag down a taxi to take you back to your hotel. The hotel room is dark except for an automatic night light in one corner. It brings to mind 1 John 1:5-7, which says, "This is the message we heard from Jesus and now declare to you: God is light, and there is no darkness in him at all. So, we are lying if we say we have fellowship with God but go on living in spiritual darkness; we are not practicing the truth. But if we are living in the light, as God is in the light, then we have fellowship with each other, and the blood of Jesus, his Son, cleanses us from all sin." Somehow, you've never seen these verses with such clarity as you do in this moment. When you switch on the room light, the convenience light goes out. Your mind is still whirling as you reflect on all that has happened—not only on this day but in the past months of your own transformation.

You contemplate the pathway you've been traveling. It hasn't been easy. In fact, the Book of James again reminds us of the necessity to consider those difficult times as "opportunities for great joy whenever your faith has been tested" (James 1:2). "God blesses those who patiently endure testing and temptation. Afterward, you know you will receive the crown of life that God has promised to those who love him." (James 1:12)

It's late. You get ready for bed and switch off the light, and the night light resumes shining. The excitement of the day melts away. *"Goodnight, Jesus. Thank you for my transformed life."*

IMMUTABLE PRINCIPLE #8: I am determined to live a consistent life of peace by maintaining positive inner language. When I fail, I will ask forgiveness and resume the new way of thinking. Peace comes from reading the Scriptures.

PRAYER: Dear Heavenly Father, thank You for protecting my mind throughout the day so I don't fall back into my old ways of thinking. I'm grateful for the transforming power of the Scriptures to set me free from my former negative way of life. I'm thankful for more opportunities to share my story with others. Thank You for each new day of protection and safety. In Jesus' holy name, amen.

Hopeful is as hopeful does.

CHAPTER 7

GET OUT OF JAIL FREE
Love, Forgiveness, Grace, Mercy and Courage

Have you ever died and been brought back to life? June, one of the writers who told her story in Chapter 1, was actually dead for twenty-eight minutes after succumbing to a seizure caused by alcohol poisoning. From the hospital that night, we were receiving impassioned pleas to pray on her behalf from her son who is on staff at our church. When her heart started beating again, she was given another chance at life. Miraculously, she suffered no brain damage. She was already being transformed by God's power when she realized what had happened. After recommitting her life to Christ, she began regularly attending our wonderful Bible-believing church. You might say she was in her own private jail until she died in that hospital. June had been released from her personal jail when she repented, and then received forgiveness and a guarantee of eternal life. There's nothing more precious than a second chance, available because of God's mercy. For years she had tried several times to free herself from her addiction to alcohol without success, and it took the drastic measures of God to set her free at last.

I am dead to many sins, but not all sins. For example, in human terms, I'm dead to the sins of robbing banks, embezzlement and many other sins. That means I would never need a get out of jail free card (forgiveness) for these transgressions. Not ever! However, I did need to be set free from my old way of thinking and my former way of life. That's not all either. My old way of thinking caused other problems too. I substituted other distractions for God's grace, forgiveness, mercy and love to cover my emotional pain. It's difficult to explain how that could possibly be when, over many years, I'd never identified it as emotional pain. And I believe that's true of countless others who try to address their pain with things of the world that don't work, while God is both willing and able to offer lasting peace. (John 4:14) Remember, the world offers many different kinds of medication—though not necessarily prescription drugs—to cover pain. My medication is often food. That immutable principle is off track for me and needs to be rewritten or at least given a commitment to be realigned.

Since Jesus is perfect, there's always going to be something to work on to become more like Him. That's not discouraging at all. It's exciting to see what God does and how He does it. I thank God in all circumstances because in every life situation, more about Christ is revealed by the power of the Holy Spirit. (Philippians 2:12-13) The process works best when we're obedient to the Holy Spirit. We will stumble at times, but we can discover a lesson within each failure that will bring us closer to Jesus if we allow it. Paul the Apostle said, "Therefore, we do not lose heart. Though outwardly we are wasting away, yet inwardly we are being renewed day by day" (2 Corinthians 4:16, NIV). That is how he describes the process of sanctification …becoming more Christlike every day.

Until I found freedom, I was held captive by the way I thought about myself. I wish it hadn't taken so long to be set free from my old way of thinking, but I'm now grateful to be free to live as God intended. If only one person is changed by my message, it will have been worth the effort to write it. Why would the Scripture say in John 8:36, "So if the Son sets you free, you are truly free" if it weren't true?

We've heard the overused cliché in the media and on commercials that freedom isn't free. It's often used to describe the country's freedom won in previous wars. But in this context, God's mercy, grace and forgiveness are completely free. Though what Christ offers is spiritual freedom, there isn't much in life that doesn't come with a cost regardless of one's spiritual convictions. Consider these scenarios:

Healthy relationships	Giving tithe/offerings
Developing a work ethic	Financial freedom
Getting an education	Commitments of any kind
Raising children	

In fact, there is a cost to every one of these and probably everything else. Think of Newton's third law: For every action (force) in nature, there is an equal and opposite reaction. In other words, if object A exerts a force on object B, then object B also exerts an equal and opposite force on object A. Paul the Apostle had another way of explaining it found in Galatians 6:7, which says, "Do not be deceived: God is not mocked, for whatever one sows, that will he also reap." I mean, really! Couldn't most things in life be related to the spiritual dimension?

Christ forgave me. The mercy, grace and love He showed me offered me brand new spiritual and emotional freedom. Did it cost me anything? No, not in the context of renewing my mind. Yes, I took the time to seek God and be in His presence. I read the Scriptures and quietly listened for the Holy Spirit. But, indeed, there was a cost—in time, to be humbled to tears, to be transparent about the transformational change in me to the Body of Christ (the local church), to endure the emotional pain of letting go of my old nature, to have an outspoken willingness to share my Jesus story and to ask forgiveness from my wife for not being the husband I am now.

If God's yoke is easy, and His burden is light (Matthew 11:30), why do we make it seem so difficult to change? I know people who say they believe some Scriptures are true, but they can't accept other Scriptures. Are we so wise that we can determine which are true and which are not when it comes to the Bible? One would have to toss out the entire Bible if even one verse is in doubt. Are we smarter than

God? Listen to the Apostle Paul when he cleared up any doubt in 2 Timothy 3:16 when he said, "All Scripture is inspired by God and is useful to teach us what is true and to make us realize what is wrong in our lives. It corrects us when we are wrong and teaches us to do what is right." The Psalmist, David, believed this, as he recorded in Psalm 33:4, when he wrote, "For the word of the Lord holds true, and we can trust everything he does."

The real issue for those who can't accept the whole counsel of Scripture is trust. The Scripture proves its reliability, but how can someone who doesn't see the Bible as a credible source have faith? They will simply have to arrive by faith (hope). "We walk by faith and not by sight" (2 Corinthians 5:7). Until that happens, it will be difficult to begin a life with Christ. All kinds of things are written about faith in the Scriptures, but "it is impossible to please God without faith. Anyone who wants to come to him must believe that God exists and that he rewards those who sincerely seek him." (Hebrews 11:6)

It's absolutely necessary to experience God through the Scriptures, with the help of the Holy Spirit, in order to have a personal relationship with Him. Remember the importance of letting the Word touch our emotions? If we walk away unchanged, it's either because we're unwilling to let the Word penetrate our hearts or because we're only casually reading the Scriptures—merely checking it off of our to-do list.

My life transformation took time. I had to discipline my mind, taking old thoughts captive (2 Corinthians 10:5) and making them obedient to my new way of thinking. It required humbling myself before God and family. (James 4:10) I had to commit to read the Scriptures (Deuteronomy 6:6-9) and train myself to hear impressions from the Holy Spirit. I had to confess that I have useful and valuable spiritual gifts given by God to be used for His glory and have a willingness to tell my Jesus story whenever a situation presents itself. I always had to be aware and answerable to walk daily with the Holy Spirit as my guide. I realize that this might seem like quite a list, but don't worry about it. Just let life unfold day by day with a willingness to be obedient to serve Jesus.

Both my wife and I grew up in farm homes with hard-working dads while our moms kept the home and reared the children. We both witnessed those very traditional male and female roles. I worked in education while my wife took care of our home and our two children. At times she would hint that she could really use some help dealing with all of her roles, but I had never seen that modeled. Though I intently focused on my career and my own challenges, I regret to say that I never complied with her requests for help. But when I was transformed, I became much more helpful. At one point, my wife exclaimed, "I have a new husband." I still haven't arrived, but at least she noticed that Jesus was in the process of changing me. Even now, sometimes she will tell me she's taking care of a task herself because she sees I'm busy with projects—writing, for example. Before I was transformed, my main problem was that I felt she was more than capable, so why not just let her handle things? Thank God, He changed my thinking.

My understanding of grace didn't happen until more recent years when I read a Charles Swindoll book, *The Grace Awakening*. It made a huge difference in my life. It helped me to cancel a great deal of shame that had built up over the years. The most incredible teaching was just how much God loved me. His grace is sufficient. God's power is now clearly evident in my life. The Scriptures prove it. The release in my spirit was so powerful that many have experienced this same power from the witness of my testimony. God's ministry through me should be at work until I'm no longer capable of doing so.

My life should be a spiritual act of worship in whatever I do. When my life isn't worship, it's likely time to ask for forgiveness.

The whole idea that I'm writing a chapter called Get Out of Jail Free would be offensive to some believers. Of course, I'm not going to throw the baby out with the bathwater. In fact, Paul asked and answered the question when he asked if we are to continue in sin that grace may abound. Of course, we are not. (Romans 6) God's grace is free, but we are not to take advantage of it. We are supposedly dead to sin or are at least making progress to reflect the character of Christ.

The Gospels teach that God's grace is enough. His grace is reflected through the Book of Psalms too. "Oh, what joy for those whose disobedience is forgiven, whose sin is put out of sight!" (Psalm 32:1) That's what mercy is. The incredible completeness comes in knowing that through Christ's blood sacrifice, my sins are completely washed away—as if I'd never sinned, if I ask for forgiveness. Here's the confirmation of just how much God loves me. "Yes, what joy for those whose record the Lord has cleared of guilt, whose lives are lived in complete honesty!" (Psalm 32:2) This was the way the love of God was described to me in a new and compelling way. It was actually Psalm 32 that played a part in completely changing my way of thinking. I call it my life chapter.

I had been in so much bondage to the feelings of inadequacy, shame and fear of rejection that the truth of Romans 5:1 could not fully penetrate my spirit. But Christ truly set me free. Now I just have to make sure that I stay free and don't get tied up again in slavery to the law. There is no reason for me to take back my old way of thinking which would result in once again being enslaved to my old way of life. I am free at last!

But what about a get out of jail free card in the context of God's grace and salvation? Romans 5:1 explains this concept best when Paul the Apostle said, "Therefore, since we have been made right in God's sight by faith, we have peace with God because of what Jesus Christ our Lord has done for us." Couldn't people take advantage of sinful living? Freedom to sin?

I have been justified—made righteous in the sight of God—and can ask forgiveness for my failures. Continual failures could potentially lead me back to being a slave to sin, and slavery is like bondage, and bondage is like jail. We are held captive to whatever we run to. Running to Christ rather than the things of this world leads us back to freedom. "My dear children, I am writing this to you so that you will not sin. But if anyone does sin, we have an advocate who pleads our case before the Father. He is Jesus Christ, the one who is truly righteous." (1 John 2:1)

The decisions we make without Jesus will eventually cause us pain when our focus is on the things of this world. God's grace and love gives us the desire to return to Him when we have sinned. "The sacrifice you desire is a broken spirit. You will not reject a broken and repentant heart, O God." (Psalm 51:17)

Romans 5:20a tells us that "God's law was given so that all people could see how sinful they were." How could God love us when we have clearly sinned? It's absolutely because of Jesus. But as people sinned more and more, God's wonderful grace became more abundant.

My hope is that I will continue to get to know God more deeply, as led by the power of the Holy Spirit. The answer to those who live outside of what the Scriptures teach, and all of us have at one time or another, is explained in James 1:22-24: "But don't just listen to God's word. You must do what it says. Otherwise, you are only fooling yourselves. For if you listen to the Word and don't obey, it is like glancing at your face in a mirror. You see yourself, walk away, and forget what you look like."

What does it mean to experience God, then, and how do you do it? God is not a formula. We all have different temperaments and gifts. How God reaches you could be completely different from the way He reached out to me. But one thing is for sure. God said in Jeremiah 29:13 that "if you look for me wholeheartedly, you will find me." Ultimately, I experienced God to a new depth of understanding and freedom by meditating on the Scriptures. (Philippians 1:6) I started spending more time getting to know God every day— specifically, just how much He loves me, how I'm forgiven and how I was created to be enough, as shown in the Scriptures. (Psalm 61:1)

It took courage to want to be transformed to a new way of thinking. We get used to life as it is, and being transformed into a whole new likeness feels unfamiliar, causes fear and, depending on circumstances, may cause personal pain. It's not uncommon to hear people say that it is too hard to live the Christian life. It's as if a person would rather be in emotional pain, which is far more difficult than accepting Jesus in a true, growing relationship.

The love of things in this world can also creep subtly into our lives. One of the biggest is idolatry. We haven't bowed down to idols or made a golden calf, but there are still idols in our modern world that can take us away from a close relationship with God. Idolatry is often rooted in selfishness and can wreak havoc with the decisions we make and how they impact others. I readily confess that, almost without fail, the problems that caused the most angst for me and others were those brought on by my own selfishness. Yet, in every single case, the selfishness resulted in confession—always to Jesus, and sometimes to those I'd wronged or sinned against. It's never fun to clean up the messes we cause, but spiritual freedom is the result of confession and forgiveness. Hopefully, this will be as huge a light bulb moment for you as it was for me. It can be a long path to freedom if there is personal resistance to change.

A pastor friend named Dan shared a story about how his personal selfishness almost got in the way of having the courage to do the right thing for his children. Pastors are people too:

"I was in my early forties and pastoring a growing church I had planted a few years earlier. I was ambitious and driven, getting more and more recognition. It was like crack cocaine to an addict!

We were breaking records, and I was getting invitations to speak at conferences. My next step was to get my doctorate, up my game, and really be ready for the next opportunity. Books were brewing in my mind, another building program was in the works, and I was on track.

Our two little kids (a boy, age five and a girl, age four) were a great joy and lots of fun for Susan and me. We really wanted children. When they finally came, we were thrilled, and I tried to spend time with them most every day. If I had an evening meeting, I would come home for two to three hours in the afternoon and make life fun for them.

But I also really wanted to get my doctorate. Many of my friends were working toward theirs, and it just sounded so right to be DOCTOR Secrist! So, I enrolled in a program and went to work. One day, I was studying at home in my den when I heard little voices and a tiny knock on the door: "Daddy, can you come play with us?"

"Well, I don't have much time but, yes." I stuck my fingers under the door and they began to giggle, grabbing my fingers. Then they stuck their little fingers under the door on my side. I pushed on them as if on piano keys, and they laughed, pulled back, and squealing, kicked the floor with their little feet. We did this for a while until I finally said, "Daddy has to study now. You kids go outside and play in the backyard." They groaned! I closed the door and, BOOM! There was a tiny knock on the door, then sixteen little fingers popped under it. I laughed, dropped to the floor and played piano keys again.

Finally, I said, "I'm serious now. I really have to study. This is it. Go play outside. I closed the door firmly and heard tiny, muffled voices on the other side. I went to my desk and sat down to my open book. A minute or two later, I glanced down at the door. There, in total silence, were sixteen tiny fingers wiggling, waiting, hoping. I was at a crossroads.

As I saw it, two major life goals were in conflict: I could sequester myself for the next four to five years and emerge as "Dr. Secrist," or I could spend time with my children in the ways of the Lord and invest those precious years in the next generation of potential Christian leaders. I was too busy to do both. But when Moses stood before the Lord, God asked him, "What is that in your hand?" It was just a stick, but it was in his hand, and it was at the ready. What

did I have in hand? I sat and pondered briefly, then went to the door.
I knew.

*"Okay, kids, let's play!" Two little faces lit up as they shouted,
"Yay!" I went outside with them and had a great, fun afternoon. I can't
remember what we did, and I'm sure they can't either, but I know I
turned a corner in my life with that one decision.*

*Over the next years, we built both church buildings and
snowmen, planted vegetable gardens and took hikes, sent out
missionaries and took missions trips, sang funny songs at home, went
camping, and baptized hundreds of new converts. Sunday was the best
day of the week, and my kids were both very involved and loved
church. Those were good, fruitful years. But I also spent time with my
children as they grew into adulthood. We helped them with homework,
worked through problems, took vacations, and enjoyed life together. I
have no regrets. Today they are both serving the Lord wholeheartedly
and both have master's degrees. They passed me up long ago, and I
am proud of them. I will never be Dr. Secrist, but today that doesn't
matter. A small decision can have big consequences."*

Dan, thanks for sharing your personal story.

How is Dan's story with his children symbolic of our
relationship with God? Spending time with God is a choice sometimes
obliterated by our selfish design for a day, let alone a lifetime. At times
we fail to realize how each day is our spiritual act of worshiping God
as our Heavenly Father. It is communion with God through
impressions from the Holy Spirit. It is feeling God's complete,
unequalled love for us. The Scriptures ask this question: "What kind
of Father would give his children a stone?" (Matthew 7:9) Dan could
have gotten his doctorate during a critical period in his children's lives
and symbolically given them a stone. But instead, he gave his children
bread—in other words, his time.

God is looking for true worshipers who "worship in spirit and
in truth" (John 4:24). Did Dan want to get his doctorate as a form of
idolatry, something that takes the place of God? Did his children learn

anything about their dad that day? Did he learn anything about himself that day? Is it possible to do the right things for the wrong reasons? All these questions have answers that only you can answer in the context of your own decisions.

I learned that sometimes I subconsciously made decisions to satisfy an emotional need that, in the end, wasn't a good thing. But I am not God. I cannot necessarily meet my emotional needs because I am not the true source of help. God is. In cases where I incessantly replayed my negative inner language over a long period of time, it was difficult to differentiate between what was truth and what was not. The clarity with which John Piper[11] explains how he keeps his emotions from spiraling out of control was as refreshing as waking to a beautiful spring day:

"My feelings are not God. God is God. My feelings do not define truth. God's Word defines truth. My feelings are echoes and responses to what my mind perceives. And sometimes—many times— my feelings are out of sync with the truth. When that happens—and it happens every day in some measure—I try not to bend the truth to justify my imperfect feelings, but rather, I plead with God: Purify my perceptions of your truth and transform my feelings so that they are in sync with the truth."

—John Piper, Bible teacher and
founder of DesiringGod.org

By now, you've noticed those immutable principles at the end of each chapter. I hope you've been taking them to heart. I actually don't care if you use those exact immutable (unchangeable) principles, but you must base yours on biblical principles of living.

Immutables are the standards by which you live. Notice I didn't say biblical standards by which you live. Whatever unchanging principles you choose to live by, biblical or not, will govern your life.

When I was working in the education field, I knew amazing students who really wanted to learn. They never caused a problem. They had loving parents who had great relationships with their children. I used to tell these kids' parents that it wouldn't matter if I tried to stop them from learning, they would still excel because of their desire to learn.

I also knew a few students who were adrift. Their parents were not supportive of school and not really connected to their children in the context of a relationship. Statistically, unsupportive parents often had a difficult time in school themselves. Their children can know they're loved, yet not have a loving, nurturing relationship with their parents.

Infrequently, our school district would offer parenting classes, but the target audience usually didn't participate. My perception is that some students had a few good standards and, at the same time, a few inconsistent and somewhat confusing standards. It didn't matter whether the standards they had were godly or not. It just mattered that the family's standards were healthy and consistent. I used to say a few students didn't have anywhere to hang their hat—meaning, no solid beliefs or framework in their lives on which to anchor their souls.

What can happen when children don't have a belief system? Where does this belief system come from? Of course, parents generally establish the family belief system —for example, acceptable behavior, responsibilities expected in the home, or some kind of faith training. Grandparents or other key adult role models might also develop a belief system. What's acceptable for one family isn't necessarily acceptable to another. But when students feel insecure because of inconsistent and unhealthy standards, it creates an uneasiness about their own well-being and sometimes even their safety.

It's no different for adults. If a belief system isn't passed on to the children, they will develop their own belief systems—sometimes good, sometimes not so good. As stated earlier, parents often pass on what was passed on to them because it's difficult to teach what you don't know.

People outside the faith may be incredibly successful, but behind their success is still a set of standards they've used to put them on a path to success. It's unavoidable. The path to success is often rooted in Christian principles anyway. Every single day I must determine to live by the immutable principles I've discovered that have brought peace to my soul.

Veering away from even one of my immutable principles might seem like a very small thing, but it's also a very subtle thing. If I were to develop a spreadsheet representing the times spent in reading and studying the Scriptures, on meditating in the presence of the Holy Spirit, and in ministry to others, you would see a direct correlation. It would show how the self-inflicted difficulties in my life have been directly related to my commitment to maintain my close relationship with God. A bar graph created from this spreadsheet would reveal the correlation between faithfulness and slowly drifting away. I've actually done this exercise in my head numerous times. It always turns out the same. Whenever I've drifted imperceptibly away from my close relationship with God, personal pain has always been the result. You see, living away from my personal standards starts with just a small decision to change my definition of faithfulness. It's almost imperceptible, but, little by little, the fellowship of the Holy Spirit is lost.

Day by day, our journey goes on with whatever immutable principles are in place. How will you make the journey?

IMMUTABLE PRINCIPLE #9: I will determine every day to live in the freedom of knowing I'm in a relationship which depends on my daily response to God. Anything less than that is a return to my old way of thinking and living.

PRAYER: My dear Heavenly Father, I pray for Your divine direction and counsel over my life so that I might live a life pleasing to You and a life of spiritual strength and safety for me. In Jesus' holy name, amen.

Hope has a name. Jesus.

CHAPTER 8

PLEASURE AND PAIN

Obeying, Trusting, Belonging, Believing and Acknowledging

We've planned several trips abroad with the help of a close relative who is an amazing vacation planner. The anticipation of those trips always brought a high degree of pleasure. Just imagining something as enjoyable as previous overseas trips has the potential to again release dopamine from my brain's pleasure center, the nucleus accumbens. This is not about brain science though. It's about recognizing how the desire for pleasure affects us.

There's no question about whether I'd rather participate in pleasure or pain. Pain is never an experience I willingly choose. Like most people, I've experienced my share of pain, sometimes as the result of my own decisions or wrong thinking about who I thought I was. Couldn't there be an easier way to learn hard lessons than through our pain? We could say pain has purpose, according to James 1:2-4 …"when troubles of any kind come your way, consider it an opportunity for great joy. For you know that when your faith is tested, your endurance has a chance to grow. So, let it grow, for when your endurance is fully developed, you will be perfect and complete, needing nothing."

I can't deny that we can learn lessons from pain. Obviously, the thoughts we have are managed by the brain. Some thoughts and activities bring pleasure, which may be realized by a dopamine release, while other thoughts are quickly discarded because we know hose thoughts will lead to pain. As I've already said, there are many sins to which we are dead, while we entertain others from time to time. My life is proof that I haven't always disposed of thoughts that led to pain. Without going into detail, let's just call them the sins of the flesh. And don't jump to the conclusion that sins of the flesh are only sexual sins. There are many others. I've already confessed to my relationship with our refrigerator and pantry. Galatians 5:19-21 contains a long list of sins of the flesh. Other references appear in the Scriptures too, but for the sake of this conversation, I have sometimes chosen without thinking the idea that my brain's pleasure center needed a boost. That is when my brain is the absolute weakest. My guard is down because I think I need a boost—a brain chemical release. If I'm not alert, I could be ripe for an attack from the father of lies, Satan. The thoughts might go something like this:

- Wouldn't it be fun to look at or experience that?
- Why don't you do this or that?
- You would get so much pleasure from it.
- No one would find out.
- No one would get hurt.
- I know you would really enjoy this idea.

Did I miss anything? How could I not be aware when this is happening? Do I see pleasure only? Is pain involved?

Spiritual warfare starts in the brain. We'll have those seemingly great ideas for generating a little mood boost. Even the bad ideas we act upon give us a hit from our brain's pleasure center. Whatever idea we act upon will often bring some kind of pleasure. "What? Do we dare to rouse the Lord's jealousy? Do you think we are stronger than he is? You say, "I am allowed to do anything"—but not everything is good for you. You say, "I am allowed to do anything"—but not everything is beneficial." (1 Corinthians 10:22-23) Some decisions we make are simply not beneficial. Pleasure is pleasure, regardless of where it comes from, but it does matter whether pleasure ends in a painful experience.

At the moment we experience pleasure, it's a great feeling—like a box of chocolates or a vanilla latte. It's just that some of the decisions I've made have led to pain. It's difficult to comprehend why a person may not be able to look far enough down the road to see the positive or negative consequences of their decisions. A person's vision is often limited and can see only the pleasure derived from moving forward with a great idea—or sometimes, a temptation. I've often reasoned and even rationalized, I deserve this. There can be just enough truth in an idea to make it appealing while the lie is hidden within it. We sometimes justify acting on wrong choices. If there was ever an example of spiritual warfare, this is it. The goal is to be spiritually dead to sin rather than fulfill the sins of the flesh that lead to spiritual death of the soul. (2 Corinthians 7:10) I try to remember to confront lies with the truth of who I really am.

That brings us back to listening to that still small voice in our heads that is called our conscience. Some might refer to that still small voice as a message from the Holy Spirit helping us to make the right choices. If the truth of God and the Scriptures will set us free, we are free, indeed (John 8:32), depending on what we are slaves to; right living known as righteousness or living according to the sins of the flesh.

Sometimes the decisions we make are based on what the mind rationalizes as good and even deserved. That kind of lie started in the Garden of Eden when Satan sold Eve on the idea her eyes would "*be opened*" as soon as she ate it, and she would "be like God, knowing both good and evil. The woman was convinced. She saw that the tree was beautiful and its fruit looked delicious, and she wanted the wisdom it would give her. So, she took some of the fruit and ate it. Then she gave some to her husband, who was with her, and he ate it, too." (Genesis 3:5-6)

Notice that Eve was persuaded to eat the forbidden fruit. She was presented with enough evidence to convince her that the pleasure of eating the fruit would satisfy a need she had. At the time of the temptation, it likely never occurred to Eve that pain would result from the additional pleasure she sought from eating the fruit.

Dopamine released in the brain is the equivalent of a powerfully addictive prescription drug. When the experience of addictive behaviors becomes too great to withstand, a wrong choice can be the equivalent of a destroyed life. Science has shown that what initially produced enough brain boost, will, over time, escalate higher and higher until it controls us.

Which seems to be more profitable—conforming to the Scriptural way of life or conforming to what the world has offered us? The pleasure or the pain? We sometimes try to live in both what the culture has offered and what God has offered us through the Scriptures. Now catch this if you can! Immeasurable pleasure comes from living a disciplined life as described in the Scriptures. I've tried to express the immense pleasure of living a life full of and led by the Holy Spirit. No other pleasure equals the pleasure given by the Holy Spirit for an obedient life. It has been and is incredibly transformational. (1 Samuel 15:22)

Yes, there certainly are acceptable earthly pleasures too. We have enjoyed incredible God-given pleasures with our family, friends and faith. Our family has tried to keep a healthy balance of earthly activities that never take the place of our love for God. Speaking of God, Psalm 16:11 reminds me, "You will show me the way of life, granting me the joy of your presence and the pleasures of living with you forever."

Both pleasure and pain have the power to convince us to take action. Think of the last time you had to be convinced of something. Maybe you had to be convinced of the deal offered when you bought a car or real estate, or when you entered into a relationship that resulted in marriage. The key word is convinced. When the evidence mounts to the level of being convinced, you move forward without hesitation.

When I became convinced of my inability to accept myself for who God created me to be, I yielded to the Scriptures and the Holy Spirit. You see, nothing can separate me from the love of God. Read it for yourself in Romans 8:38-39. You'll note that you are included in the promise. That can be transformational. Let it be the beginning of changing the way you think (Romans 12:1-2).

When I was a young boy growing up in eastern Washington, I used to think people in our part of the state were more intelligent, more talented, and able to problem solve better than people in western Washington. After all, we were self-sustaining farmers and problem solvers. I watched my dad who could fix anything. He even designed and built tools to solve challenging problems. As a child who hadn't yet been to Seattle, I believed we had to be more gifted than those "westies" because they probably didn't have opportunities to develop problem-solving skills like we did on the farm.

Of course, I grew out of that way of thinking as I matured. When we moved to western Washington many years later, I had to laugh when I recalled my old ways of thinking. There really are gifted and talented people here—lots of them. If I hadn't been convinced before, I certainly was later on. It's that kind of thing where your mind gets tipped over by the evidence. Once we're convinced to live as God intended us to live, we'll see the new truth of how much pleasure results in being a Christ follower.

It's being convinced that helped me to move forward in God's grace and love for me. Let the truth of the Scriptures convince you. Meditate on them. Read them over many times. Take care of your soul. Develop a sense of gratitude for the work of the Holy Spirit in your life.

During the months I've spent writing this book, especially during the last two chapters, I've experienced considerable spiritual warfare from the forces of darkness—Satan and his angels. How could

I possibly be worthy enough or smart enough or capable enough of writing to take on this project? Yet, I couldn't get away from the idea of sharing what was happening within me. The Holy Spirit just kept confronting me with the message until I said *yes* to writing. I've had to rebuke those lies in the name of Jesus and remember that the Scriptures say I'm God's masterpiece (Ephesians 2:10). I must also remember all the times I've helped others through their difficult circumstances, and that equals motivation for my purpose. My purpose could be fulfilled or destroyed by the choices I make. I must persevere.

Part of my transformation was realizing that I am in Christ, and Christ is in me. God has united us with Christ Jesus. "For our benefit God made him to be wisdom itself. Christ made us right with God; he made us pure and holy, and he freed us from sin." (1 Corinthians 1:30) That's what I call abiding in Jesus. We become an abiding part of Jesus through the power of the Holy Spirit because He lives within our being. "For his Spirit joins with our spirit to affirm that we are God's children." (Romans 8:16)

To be in communion and relationship with Jesus through the power of the Holy Spirit means I abide in Christ every day. I do not waiver. Psalm 16:7-8 sets a pattern for daily living. "I will bless the Lord who guides me; even at night my heart instructs me. I know the Lord is always with me. I will not be shaken, for he is right beside me." Even when trials come, my faith and trust in Jesus are like a solid rock.

"When you obey my commandments, you remain in my love, just as I obey my Father's commandments and remain in his love." (John 15:10). That's why daily abiding in God's love helps us to persevere in His presence. The pleasure or the pain? (Deuteronomy 30:19)

A law is created to resolve a problem. A law on the books is locked in. It's immutable. But in life, a resolution to the way we think or to change any part of our spiritual life is determined by obedience.

At first, it's hard work until your spirit is convinced of your need to change.

The battle of the mind will continue. Every day, even when there is the temptation to wrongly engage in a sin of the flesh, I must be determined to win against temptation. My goal is to be obedient to each immutable principle established in my life to keep me spiritually strong, and to keep me from reverting back to my old way of thinking.

My ministry to others will be determined by obedience to the biblical principles in my life. "How joyful are those who fear the Lord—all who follow his ways! You will enjoy the fruit of your labor. How joyful and prosperous you will be!" (Psalm 128:1-2)

I must guard my life every day because whether I do or not will determine my course in life. When temptation occurs, it's important to stop and think. I have to figure out ways to remove obstacles to spiritual health so I can keep my life on track. If I don't, I make it difficult for God to accomplish what He planned for me to do long ago. The pleasure or the pain?

Knowing about God and experiencing God through the power of the Holy Spirit are two different things. Allow yourself to be used to help those whom God places in your life. Let your life emanate the love of Jesus. Your life should be a spiritual act of worship. (Romans 12:1)

Scriptures teach us in 2 Corinthians 10:5 to take our thoughts captive when temptation comes. Again, in order to take our thoughts captive, we have to change the way we think as demonstrated in Philippians 4:8 "And now, dear brothers and sisters, one final thing. Fix your thoughts on what is true, and honorable, and right, and pure, and lovely, and admirable. Think about things that are excellent and worthy of praise." We take control of our minds by thinking like this. There is pleasure in knowing we may have just avoided pain caused from replaying or embracing powerful thoughts capable of destroying us. We must look past the initial pleasure of an idea to discern whether it's from God or our enemy, Satan. To act on any sinful decision will ield pleasure that is short lived—temporary. Pain caused by a poor decision can last a lifetime. "You will keep in perfect peace all who trust in you, all whose thoughts are fixed on you!" (Isaiah 26:3)

Get ready to rumble. Let's talk about football. Don't laugh. We've been watching the Seahawks for years, even though I have no gift for sports. I know many but not all of the rules of football, though I would not be qualified to be a Monday morning quarterback. We could call the rules of football the immutable principles required for the game. In the NFL, there are those dreaded penalties when a professional player doesn't adhere to the rules of the game. A fifteen-yard penalty might result from a costly mistake. There's a price to pay in the NFL if the player continues to make costly mistakes. It could result in a career change.

What about NFL coaches? One NFL coach decided to solicit a prostitute on the eve of the Super Bowl. Think about the thought process this coach may have gone through. Perhaps he was feeling anxious about the game. He may have felt he needed a boost from his pleasure center without thinking past the pleasure to see the pain he might also experience. The mind can rationalize and sometimes deceive us. That's why establishing immutable principles grounded in biblical faith is so important to our spiritual strength.

If we drive a vehicle, we adhere to the rules of the road. Once in a while, we might go over the speed limit or run a red light. Sometimes, we might not get caught, while other times we might get a ticket. What about those traffic cams that are in intersections snapping a photo and capturing video of our misdeed? We mostly remember all the rules for driving, but sometimes we fail. We might even get into an accident if we're not observant. The goal is to adhere to the immutable principles of driving. The more we do, the safer we'll be.

We might say the degree of pain we go through has a controlling influence on us. It has a way of convincing us. Throughout my life, there were times when the pain I experienced wasn't too difficult. Pain's influence might be short-lived. I might even make the same decision again if the pain has completely been forgotten. Other experiences were so difficult that the situation convinced me I had to change to avoid a repeat of that kind of pain. It just wasn't worth it.

We seem to keep immutable principles for all kinds of things in life without much thought. They're just there. It stands to reason that our spiritual life requires a set of principles to protect us as well.

The things we've talked about at the end of each chapter should be a natural part of life. You can also make your own unchanging principles, provided they are within biblical guidelines. We sometimes forget, but the goal is to remember more and more who we are as believers and forget less and less. After all, the goal is to make us more clearly reflect the character of Christ. Without taking care of our spiritual life, we will face self-inflicted pain. I've experienced failure, and I have learned from those failures.

Self-inflicted pain happens when we make poor decisions outside the experience, good sense and rules of the game of life. I challenge the reader to think of anything in life that doesn't have a set of principles that govern it.

Years ago, on my dad's farm, the spring winds always blew tumbleweeds across his fields. As they blew across the fields, those tumbleweeds would leave a trail of seeds wherever the wind blew them. In order to reap a powerful harvest, my dad would plant the wheat seeds in narrow orderly rows. On the other hand, those tumbleweeds scattered unintended seeds wherever they landed. The unintended seeds yielded no harvest and no value to my dad. The life cycle of both intended and unintended seeds continues until they are interrupted. This made me think about the unintended seeds I've planted in my own life. These seeds sprang up and tried to choke out the good things I'd planted. I had to clean up my "field" so the good seeds would thrive and destroy the unintended bad seeds. Hosea 10:12 reminded me of the kind of seed that I should always plant. "I said, 'Plant the good seeds of righteousness, and you will harvest a crop of love. Plow up the hard ground of your hearts, for now is the time to seek the LORD, that he may come and shower righteousness upon you.'"

In my old way of thinking, I planted many seeds of doubt. The barely visible seeds of inadequacy were unintended in the sense that I didn't know what was truly bothering my spirit. But now I am convinced of my true self as I was created by God. The intended seeds I plant from day to day are the intended seeds of righteousness (Godly, right living) to be a harvest of love. Doing so will bring intended joy to my life as I serve others.

That brings us to the whole point of this writing. I want you to:

- know the joy living in God's pleasure and avoid sin's pain.
- take care of your soul by making good decisions based on the Scriptures as your source of spiritual food.
- have a deeper understanding of who God created you to be.
- love God in a new way with a deeper understanding of His grace.
- develop consistent biblical standards that offer spiritual strength and safety.
- be able to help others as the opportunity presents itself.
- acknowledge your God-given gifts and talents, then offer them in service to others.
- trust and believe the power of God through the Holy Spirit to change you in accordance with His plan for you.

I am writing this book with passion and love for the reader. This book is not just about me. It's about those of us who desire to live a new life of biblical freedom and service to others. I am no longer paralyzed by my boyhood thoughts of comparison and being less than others. I am enough. You are enough. May my purpose help to develop your purpose.

IMMUTABLE PRINCIPLE #10: I will live in the freedom of knowing how much Jesus loves me and gave His life for me. There is great understanding that there is now no condemnation to those who are in Christ Jesus (Romans 8:1), and that nothing can separate me from God's love because of the death and resurrection of Jesus. (Romans 8:38-39)

PRAYER: Dear Heavenly Father, I pray that You, the source of hope, will fill me completely with joy and peace because I trust in You. Please help me to overflow with confident hope through the power of the Holy Spirit. (Romans 15:13) In Jesus' holy name, amen.

"But you, dear friends, must build each other up in your most holy faith, pray in the power of the Holy Spirit, and await the mercy of our Lord Jesus Christ, who will bring you eternal life. In this way, you will keep yourselves safe in God's love." (Jude 1:20-21)

I am who He says I am.

ENDNOTES

* Google Earth, Denmark School, Kittitas County, WA Imagery Date: 7/2012   46°56'07.09"N 120°24'01.09"W elevation 1663 ft eye alt 1611 ft

CHAPTER 1

[1]The Forgotten Way, Author, Ted Dekker. Outlaw Studios, Publisher. Used by written permission.

CHAPTER 2

[2]Taken from The Bondage Breaker: Overcoming *Negative Thoughts *Irrational Feelings *Habitual Sins by Neil Anderson. Copyright © 2000 by Neil Anderson. Harvest House Publishers. Used by written permission.

[3]Robert Morris, Pastor, Gateway Church, Southlake, TX. Used by written permission.

[4]Intervarsity Press (ivpress.com). Used by written permission.

CHAPTER 3

[5]Taken from Purpose Driven Life: What On Earth Am I Here For, by Rick Warren. Copyright © 2002 by Rick Warren. Used by written permission of Zondervan. www.zondervan.com

[6]A Defense of the Christian Religion, Pensées, Blaise Pascal, 1670. Public Domain.

[7]Bob Goff, Author. Quote used by written permission.

[8]The Forgotten Way, Author, Ted Dekker. Outlaw Studios, Publisher. Used by written permission.

CHAPTER 4
[9]Brené Brown, research professor, University of Houston, Brené Brown, PhD, LMSW, Used by written permission.

CHAPTER 5
[10]Hope Has A Name. Words and music by Benjamin Cruse, Evan John, Aaron Johnson, and Ryan Williams. (Title only)

CHAPTER 7
[11]John Piper, John Piper Ministries, DesiringGod.org. Used by written permission.

ACKNOWLEDGEMENTS

God, the Father, God, the Son, & God, the Holy Spirit

Special thanks to the six writers who contributed to
this work by sharing their own personal story.

Mike Johnson, Ph.D. & Tami Johnson for valuable insight into
storytelling and connection to others

My parents, Keith & Doris Johnson for the gift of music

The readers who provided valuable feedback on each chapter

Tamara Richardt & Cristina Smith
Writing Coaches—Get Published Now

Cover Design by 99Designs.com Anointing Productions

Author Photography by Bob Rowan

Illustrations and Images

Google Maps • Page 4 • Used by permission.
Leon Johnson school photo • Page 4 • Unknown photography
Farm house • Page 6 • Family photo
Leon Johnson • Page 7 • Provided by parents
Rhythm Sticks • Page 8 • Provided by Denise Sievers
Bucket Images • Page 55 • by Leon Johnson
Piano Album • Page 61 • Photography by Bob Rowan
Young Boy Image • Page 70 • by Leon Johnson
Wedding Image • Page 72 • Burchett's Studio • Spokane, WA
Our Children • Page 73 • Family Photo

About the Author

Over the years of his career, Leon saw a pattern not only in other children, but in himself. One discovery after another led him to a clear and miraculous epiphany that allowed him to break free from past inner childhood language and adopt new language consistent with the promises of God.

Author Leon Johnson is a life-long learner, retired teacher, principal, and special programs administrator. His experience spans a thirty-four-year career followed by another fifteen years spent studying child development. Leon also supervised student teacher practicums for Pacific Lutheran University in Tacoma, Washington. He is an accomplished pianist, having released his first album in 2019. He earned a BA and MA from Central Washington University and advanced administrative credentials from both Central and Eastern Washington Universities.

Leon has been married to his beautiful wife, Tana for forty-five years. They have two grown children and their spouses, and five grandchildren. The joy of faith and family is unsurpassed.

Other Available Products and Services

Seminar speaker and teacher upon request

Discussion Guide
eBook
Audiobook
4-CD Audio Set

Made in the USA
Monee, IL
13 March 2021